When meeting Muslims, can we interact ho
graciously testify to the life, death and lordsh
encounters, this book provides models. The
And they are more specific than those in most other books. Beyond Beards and
Burqas *is a useful guide for Christians who want to love their neighbours.*

Miriam Adeney, PhD
Associate Professor of Global and Urban Ministries,
Seattle Pacific University
Teaching Fellow, Regent College

Insightful and overflowing with warmth and compassion, Beyond Beards and
Burqas *is an ideal introduction for Christians who want to learn more about
Muslims and Islam. Drawing upon decades of experience, Martin explores
the rich variety of beliefs and practices behind what we often perceive as a
monolithic Islam, and helps the reader think through numerous starting points
for sharing Christ with our Muslim friends.*

Andy Bannister
Visiting Lecturer, Oxford Centre for Christian Apologetics

*This is vintage Goldsmith! Martin and his wife Elizabeth have lived and worked
among Muslims in South East Asia for many years, and, as the stories in this
book demonstrate, there's hardly a country with a Muslim presence that they
haven't visited at one time or another. Martin has studied and taught Islam
in many different contexts, and therefore knows Islam at its best and as it
actually is. Everything that he writes is rooted in his personal experience and
his encounters with Muslims of many different kinds. In addition to all this,
he writes so clearly and with the kind of humour which all who know him will
instantly recognize. This unique combination of gifts and qualifications makes
this a wonderfully readable book with a powerful message that needs to be heard
by Christians today.*

Colin Chapman
Former Lecturer in Islamic Studies, Near East School of Theology,
Beirut, Lebanon,
Author of *Cross and Crescent: Responding to the Challenges of Islam* (IVP)

Some names and details of the conversations in this book have been altered for reasons of security.

Martin Goldsmith

Beyond
beards & burqas

Connecting with Muslims

ivp

INTER-VARSITY PRESS
Norton Street, Nottingham NG7 3HR, England
Email: ivp@ivpbooks.com
Website: www.ivpbooks.com

© Martin Goldsmith 2009

Martin Goldsmith has asserted his right under the Copyright, Design and Patents
Act, 1988, to be identified as Author of this work.

All rights reserved. No part of this publication may be reproduced, stored in a
retrieval system, or transmitted, in any form or by any means, electronic, mechani-
cal, photocopying, recording or otherwise, without the prior permission of the
publisher or the Copyright Licensing Agency.

Unless otherwise stated, Scripture quotations are taken from the Holy Bible, New
International Version. Copyright © 1973, 1978, 1984 by International Bible Society.
First published in Great Britain 1979. Used by permission of Hodder & Stoughton
Ltd, a member of Hodder Headline Group. All rights reserved. 'NIV' is a registered
trademark of International Bible Society. UK trademark number 1448790.

First published 2009

British Library Cataloguing in Publication Data
A catalogue record for this book is available from the British Library.

ISBN 978–1–84474–410–7

Set in Monotype Dante 12/15pt
Typeset in Great Britain by Servis Filmsetting Ltd, Stockport, Cheshire
Printed and bound in Great Britain by Ashford Colour Press Ltd, Gosport,
Hampshire

*Inter-Varsity Press publishes Christian books that are true to the Bible and that communi-
cate the gospel, develop discipleship and strengthen the church for its mission in the world.*

*Inter-Varsity Press is closely linked with the Universities and Colleges Christian Fellowship,
a student movement connecting Christian Unions in universities and colleges throughout
Great Britain, and a member movement of the International Fellowship of Evangelical
Students. Website: www.uccf.org.uk*

CONTENTS

INTRODUCTION

Southampton to Singapore: April 1960

Our missionary life began in luxury, and also with humour, for we were due to sail from Southampton to Singapore on April Fool's Day! Joking comments flowed about the folly of committing ourselves to long-term missionary work in far-off South-east Asia.

But the British captain of the ship was not amused. His superstitious fear compelled him to refuse to set sail on such an inauspicious date, and we duly waited until 2 April. Right at the outset of our missionary careers, therefore, we learned that superstition can go hand in hand together with advanced professional training and learning. It does not infect just the uneducated.

Air travel was not yet available for ordinary people, so our group of thirty-five new missionaries, including myself and Elizabeth, from various countries of Europe and North America looked forward to three luxurious weeks aboard the magnificent P&O liner. Of course, as missionaries, our cramped cabins lay far down in the hold. Excitedly we explored the various decks and the whole layout of the ship. I knew the ship, the *SS Carthage*, already because I had travelled on it before when returning to England from Bermuda at the end of the Second World War. In those days it had served as a troop carrier, but we civilians were graciously allowed also to travel back to England with her. The Government had been aware that British children needed to be brought back as soon as possible in order to enter English schools and adapt to English education.

What exhilaration and excitement filled us! The crowds of family and friends stood waving on the quayside as the *Carthage* hooted from its funnel and slowly slipped its moorings. Gradually we left Southampton and England behind, and moved into the English Channel, setting off for our great adventure.

The choppy seas of the Bay of Biscay gave way to the calm beauty of land as we progressed through the narrow waterway between North Africa and Gibraltar. In those days, holiday travel was very restricted and none of us had ever seen the beautiful warm waters of the Mediterranean. Television had not yet burst on to the scene, so we had never seen pictures of these countries. In those days they thus seemed utterly remote and their very names rang with romantic imagery. We could almost smell the exotic fascination of Egypt and the Suez Canal with sailing boats on the nearby waterways looking as if they were moving across the desert. As we docked to refuel in Port Said and Aden, we were shocked by the dirty, unmade streets and the evident poverty. We longed for the gospel to penetrate widely in that whole area.

So we progressed for our next port of call across the Indian Ocean to Bombay (now called Mumbai) where we were greeted by missionary relatives of Elizabeth's. We much enjoyed a day ashore, sightseeing and strolling in the beauty of the famous botanical gardens.

Here I had my first experience of relating to people of a very different culture. The Indian friend who was kindly showing us the sights of Bombay was unexpectedly arrested by the police! He was falsely accused of acting as a tourist guide without proper certification. He was scared stiff and I therefore offered to accompany him to the police station. As we were led off by the police, he quietly took my hand

and we walked away hand in hand. In England, heterosexual men do not normally walk holding hands, but in many Asian cultures, this is quite normal. I felt somewhat embarrassed, knowing that all my Western missionary friends would be watching.

Those days at sea were indeed times of leisurely holiday and delightful luxury. As a group we met together each morning for a time of Bible study and open prayer. During the day we sat around in little groups, chatting and eating the ice cream which was regularly brought round by the ship's stewards. Deck games and a swimming pool gave further entertainment. The ship's meals were splendid and even our youthful appetites were more than satisfied with the abundance of superb courses. During these days together we formed close relationships, overcoming the cultural differences between us – Swiss and German, American and Canadian, English, Irish, Scottish and Welsh. So began the learning process of understanding people of another background. Of course, we would have to overcome much greater cultural hurdles later when we scattered to start our missionary careers in Japan, the Philippines, Indonesia and other Asian countries.

I had fallen in love with Elizabeth while we were still in training in England, so I rejoiced in the opportunity of being with her throughout those lovely weeks on the ship. In each port I would at some stage take the opportunity of asking her to marry me – we now wonder whether we should be in the *Guinness Book of Records* because I asked her to marry me in so many countries while she resolutely said 'no' in each port!

From Bombay we progressed down to Ceylon (now Sri Lanka) and Colombo for our next stop, where we could enjoy a balmy tropical evening walking along the seashore.

We had previously dropped into their parliament just in time to hear a motion of no confidence and to witness the fall of the Government there. On we went to Penang in Malaysia and our first encounter with Buddhist and Hindu temples. Finally the ship docked in Singapore, where we were warmly welcomed by our mission leaders.

In our first few days in Singapore, we all met with the mission leaders individually to determine which countries we should work in. It seemed right both to the directors and to me that I should be sent to Indonesia to work in and under the huge growing churches of that largely Muslim country.

In those days it often took several years to get a visa for Indonesia. It seemed obvious that I should learn Malay meanwhile and work among the Malay people. The Malay and Indonesian languages are very similar, being closely related. So I set out on the formidable task of language learning, with the prospect of changing into Indonesian when the visa eventually came.

In Singapore the traditional, strongly Muslim Malays form a significant minority in what is otherwise a largely Chinese city. But I knew nothing of Islam. I had never before met a Muslim, for back in the 1950s there were practically no Muslims in England. At my evangelical Anglican theological college, the syllabus failed to include anything related to other faiths, for in those days they were irrelevant for ministry in England. The great majority of my fellow students were heading for Anglican ordained ministry in England, so the teaching was clearly and rightly fitted to their needs. Little did the staff realize that soon Britain would become multi-ethnic and multireligious. Ministers in Britain would urgently need a good understanding of other faiths and how to communicate the good news of Jesus Christ cross-culturally.

I nevertheless found myself thrust into pioneer evangelism among Malay Muslims. While studying the language with a Malay Muslim teacher and trying to help each week in evangelism in the crowded night markets,[1] it was soon impressed upon me that my Western biblical and theological knowledge was quite inadequate for relating with Muslims and sharing the gospel relevantly with them.

Happily God had put me into a position where I could learn about Islam and Muslims, like a train running simultaneously on two parallel tracks. On the one hand I had the opportunity of meeting Muslims personally through the night markets, visiting them in their own homes in the Malay areas of the city and playing badminton with them each evening. This allowed me to ask questions, watch their behaviour, listen to their conversation and see the practice of Islam in their daily lives.

At the same time I got hold of a translation of the Qur'an in English, read it and studied it. I did not find it at all easy to read and was often tempted to stop halfway, but I was deeply aware of the need to read it carefully. Books on Islam both by Christians and also by Muslims followed on my reading list.

As is also the case with other religions, the more academic study of Islam through books helps enormously in one's understanding of what people believe and practise. But it also has to be said that what Muslims actually think and do may vary considerably from the officially accepted Islam. And like Christianity or any other faith, Islam varies from culture to culture. The books on Islam generally describe a Middle Eastern and Arab form, but Muslims in Singapore, Malaysia and Indonesia are rather different.

So book study went hand in hand with grass-roots interaction with Muslim friends and contacts. One can only be grateful for such an opportunity.

Today in the twenty-first century, library book shelves groan under the multitude of books on Islam from every perspective and angle. In such books we all have a wonderful aid to the study of Islam. I do not wish to attempt to add yet another such book. My aim is rather to share some of the very personal encounters I have enjoyed with a rich variety of Muslims, both in Britain and overseas, in the nearly fifty years that have followed this first missionary journey. It is my hope and prayer that readers may gain some further insight into and understanding of their Muslim neighbours and friends, the practice of their faith and how we can share the good news of Jesus Christ attractively with them.

Reflect

How could you make contact with local Muslims and learn about Islam from them?

As you learn about Muslims from the media, what impressions are you gaining? Do you feel that the media has a bias in relation to Islam? If so, in what direction?

1. HAJI AHMED: CAN WE KNOW GOD?

A highlight of the All Nations Islamics Course that December was the morning's lectures by a leading Muslim scholar. On the course we had a few students who were quite inexperienced in relating to Muslims, although the majority were already involved in active mission among Muslims either in Britain or overseas. It seemed right to brief them for the coming of our visitor, Haji Ahmed.

'I am sure that we shall all be challenged by the Muslim emphasis on the priority of religious duties over all other everyday activities,' I started, and then gave a personal example to illustrate this. I told them of an occasion in Tunisia when my wife and I were staying in a small guesthouse. At breakfast I was in the middle of saying grace when I observed the waiter coming to take our orders for tea or coffee. I immediately interrupted my prayer in order to tell him what we wanted for breakfast. 'We're in a Muslim context where prayer is more important than ordering tea or coffee,' my wife had reminded me afterwards. 'You should have completed your prayer and the waiter would happily have held on. As a Muslim he would have appreciated that nothing takes precedence over prayer.' She was right.

We had faced a similar situation when travelling on a bus in North Africa. At the prayer time the bus stopped and everyone got out to pray. The midday sun blazed inexorably down on us all and my wife looked desperately for some shade. But the bus's passengers had other things to fill their minds. They all had their prayer mats with them and immediately unrolled them on the dusty roadside. They then began their prayer ritual together. What should we do? Fearing that we would underline the common belief that Christians do not pray, we got our Bibles out and also prayed. But we felt our weakness in not having an obvious external ritual to show that we were praying too.

'In Islam the outward forms of their religious practice are vitally important,' I reminded the students, 'whereas Western Christians sometimes react against what seems to them to be mere ritual formality. But actually we all inevitably develop particular bodily postures when we pray.' The students laughed and nodded their heads as I continued, 'Some kneel reverently, others raise their hands in worship or dance to show their joy in the Lord. Actually, the Bible underlines how God instructs his people to develop visible symbols to stand alongside his Word in reminding us of God's promises and commands.'

It seemed right at that stage to give some more biblical teaching on this subject. 'The supreme example must be the temple itself, the manifestation to Israel of the presence of God in their midst. But numerous lesser examples can be quoted – building altars in significant places, binding sections of God's Word to the body and placing it at the entrance to the home, dressing in particular ways to keep prayer before one's eyes. The particular structure of churches can also play a part in teaching God's people. Thus some denominations have a threefold structure in the front; the Lord's table is in the centre with the reading lectern and the pulpit on either side. Other churches may have a large screen prominent in the front with the band beneath it, underlining the central role of worship in song. And of course the festivals of Israel and the Christian sacraments of baptism and the Lord's Supper are vital visual aids in reminding God's people of the central truths of our faith.'

I felt it important that the students should appreciate

how our visitor would view religion through his particular Muslim eyes, so I tried to underline the Muslim externalistic approach. 'As in Judaism, so also in Islam it is believed that faith will stem from or at least be influenced by outward actions. The New Testament, on the other hand, emphasizes that sin comes from the heart and it is our inmost being which determines our whole life. Perhaps there is truth in both. What we are will direct what we do, but it is also true that what we do influences what we are. In Islam the continual outward action of prostration in prayer plays a significant part in shaping the faith and attitudes of many Muslims.'

It was important at this stage to be more specific. 'Likewise the compulsory giving of zakat [alms] induces a concern for the poor and for orphans – we remember that Muhammad was himself an orphan, so this is important in Islam. Fasting during Ramadan reminds Muslims of the need for self-sacrificial worship of Allah, also of the importance of caring for those who lack the basics of daily life. Pilgrimage to Mecca brings home to Muslims the central role of Muhammad in their faith and they will also experience the unity of God's people as they join the vast crowds in the various rituals of the hajj. And the immense throng of pilgrims also instils a triumphant sense of Islam's superior power and truth.'

Haji Ahmed arrived in good time for a cup of coffee before his lectures. His slender body was neatly dressed in traditional Muslim attire. His brown face was softened by a gentle smile which came easily and frequently into his expression. His deep-set dark eyes lacked the sparkle of any exuberant enjoyment of his life and faith, but they met my eyes with an easy composure which revealed his quiet confidence in God and himself as a man of God. He showed no sign of any embarrassment at being in the alien context of a Christian college and in the midst of a group of actively mission-minded Christians. But having been on pilgrimage to Mecca several times, he was proud of his title 'Haji' and liked to be addressed in this way.

In his lectures the haji helpfully elaborated on some of the issues facing British Muslims. We were all impressed at his openness in sharing very practical problems. He told us how difficult it was to fast during Ramadan when daylight hours were particularly long at some times in England. What would happen if Muslims penetrated even into the far reaches of northern Scandinavia with an Arctic winter and the never-setting sun of the summer? If Ramadan were in the winter, would they fast only for such a short period each day? Or if Ramadan fell in the summer, would they fast almost the whole day long for the full month? I wondered. It is not easy to transpose laws made in and fitted to Arabia when one lives elsewhere. How good that the Christian faith does not have such detailed laws which depend so heavily on the local climate or culture, I thought to myself.

Haji Ahmed was not a brilliant communicator, but his obvious charm and sincerity carried us all with him. We felt we were meeting with Islam at its very best. At the end of his lectures he graciously opened himself to questions. Before he came, the students had been warned not to use such question times for witness and certainly not to attack Islam in any way. Good questions ensued from the students and the haji answered them with a candour that won our hearts.

'I think I know Christianity quite well,' he affirmed at one stage. 'I have read the New Testament several times and I think I have generally understood what it is saying.' He certainly gave everyone the impression that this was true. He did seem to have a good knowledge of the Christian faith. He went on to tell us, 'I have many Christian friends and we are constantly sharing about Islam and Christianity, discussing both faiths and how we personally experience them.'

Then he raised big questions in our minds when he confessed to us, 'But there is one thing which my Christian friends keep saying and which I cannot at all understand. I have asked them repeatedly what they mean, but I never get an adequate explanation. So I still cannot comprehend what they actually mean.'

We all wondered what this could be. He then explained, 'They keep saying that they know God personally. That is surely an impossibility. What do they really mean?' He went on to explain that he obeyed and served God, he sought to follow God's will, he prayed to God and knew that God heard and responded to his prayers. 'I know that God is merciful to his people and that includes me and my family,' he concluded. But the concept of an intimate personal relationship with almighty God remained beyond his understanding and experience. Sadly he felt that none of his Christian friends had been able to explain how we can know God in such a personal way nor how we can experience this relationship in daily life.

We all longed to be able to share with the haji our knowledge of God. Of course we can only come to know God through Jesus Christ by his Holy Spirit. The wonder of the Christian faith is that we have not only the gloriously holy God who is invisible (Colossians 1:15), high above mere sinful human beings. This is the emphasis also found in Islam. As Christians, with our knowledge of God in his nature as a Trinity, as well as the God on high we also have God here with us as Immanuel, walking hand in hand with us through life. We also know that God lives in us by his Spirit to give us his power in daily life and ministry. Happily, with the Trinity, we can glory in the reality that this almighty God of burning holiness also comes down to dwell with us in the person of his Son Jesus Christ and to live in us by his Spirit. As a result we can indeed 'know God personally'.

After his lectures I invited the haji to join us all for lunch with other staff and students, but he immediately apologized. 'I am afraid I am late for our prayer time. May I go somewhere quiet so that I can do my salat [the ritual prayer performed five times a day]? Then perhaps we could go together for lunch.'

So Haji Ahmed and I withdrew to my study so that he could perform his prayers. 'Which is the direction of Mecca?' he immediately asked. I was somewhat unsure, but pointed quickly in the approximate direction and hoped he would accept it. He set his face towards Mecca and began his prayers. It was a joy and privilege for me to meditate briefly on a short passage of the Bible and turn this into prayer, so that he was not alone in his devotions and there might be an obvious companionship as we both sought to please God.

Haji Ahmed and I joined the others slightly late for lunch, feeling the reality of God through our prayer time. The performance of salat five times a day may seem formal and ritualistic to many Christians, but it helps people to keep God in their hearts throughout the day.

Through this personal act of performing his prayers, Haji Ahmed symbolically represented the whole community of Islam with its emphasis on the right performance of the outward forms of their faith in obedience to the commands of Allah. Although as Christians we may reject this emphasis on outward forms as legalistic and lacking freedom, we must also admire the genuine sincerity and obedient dedication to the perceived will of Allah. It presents Western Christians with a challenge and rebuke in our more casual approach to discipleship.

After lunch and coffee with the students, Haji Ahmed

and I enjoyed a short walk round the beautiful grounds of the college. The handsome red-brick house with its ornate chimneys formed the ideal background to the lawn and woods in front. I explained that Sir Thomas Fowell Buxton, the first owner of the house, had worked with Wilberforce in the campaign to outlaw slavery. Both men were products of the evangelical revival in the first half of the 1800s.

Conversation quickly turned to the topic of the Trinity. 'As you know, our Islamic faith is centred on the great truth of the doctrine of *Tawhid*, the oneness of Allah,' Haji Ahmed started. 'I cannot understand how Christians can really believe that the one God is also somehow three. Your teaching sounds to me quite blasphemous – the one God cannot at the same time be three.'

With such an intelligent and knowledgeable Muslim, I knew that I could not avoid this difficult subject. Many Christians find the Trinity difficult to explain. And many Christian ministers dread Trinity Sunday when they have to preach on the Trinity. I sympathized with them as I strolled through the woods with my new Muslim friend.

'I'm afraid that the Christian church has failed badly in relation to the Trinity,' I confessed. 'The first Christians struggled with your precise questions. They came from a strongly monotheistic background like Jews, but then their experience of Jesus and of the Holy Spirit led them to understand that these too were God. As a result the early Christians had to struggle to explain how all three could be God and yet still retain their strong belief in one God. Eventually they came up with brilliant formulations concerning the Trinity and the divine humanity of Jesus the Messiah. But sadly these were expressed in the Greek philosophical terms of that time. People today don't think in that way and we Christians have generally failed to find more up-to-date ways of expressing what we believe.'

Haji Ahmed was clearly not impressed by what I said, so I decided to be very direct. Knowing that this could easily break our relationship, I hesitated. But I remembered how he had told us of his frequent debates with Christian friends. He had given a clear impression that he enjoyed and appreciated such open religious discussion. So I took my courage in my hands and continued, 'It seems to me that any religion which only believes in a non-trinitarian monotheism rather than a Trinity will have grave problems.'

Haji Ahmed was clearly surprised and shocked, but I decided to continue this somewhat confrontational way of defending Christian truth. I hoped that the beauty of the woods through which we were strolling might reduce any bad feeling which could arise. The thick carpet of fallen leaves with a shimmering layer of frost under the bare trees stretched as far as the eye could see.

'You may remember that early Muslim philosophers noted that God is described as all-knowing and all-seeing,' I started. 'They asked themselves what God knew and saw when he alone existed. What did God know and see before even the uncreated Qur'an or the spirit of Muhammad existed, before the universe was created? As you know, some suggested that God saw and knew himself, while others disallowed this because it assumed a duality in the godhead – one aspect of God which was known and seen, another aspect which knew and saw. But they all agreed that it is dangerous for Muslims to suggest any duality in Allah, for it is then only a short step to a Trinity.'

Haji Ahmed nodded unwillingly and exclaimed that God is great and cannot be easily explained or understood. We agreed, happily. I felt the good relationship between us had been restored, although a hint of tension hung in the air. I was conscious that the greatest sin in Islam is *Shirk* – putting anything or anybody on a level with Allah. My words had hinted at the fact that as Christians we believe that Jesus Christ and the Holy Spirit are within the godhead. To Haji Ahmed, this smacked of *Shirk* and he was on his guard.

As we walked, we startled two pheasants, which flew noisily into the air with wings flapping. 'Allah is uniquely great,' the haji reaffirmed, as if to counteract the disturbance of the pheasants. 'As Muslims we stand strongly on the unquestionable truth of the *Tawhid* of Allah.' Again we happily agreed, for both the Qur'an and the Bible declare this foundational reality that God is one.

The haji began to relax for a moment, so I took the opportunity of reminding him that many mosques have the name of Muhammad next to the name Allah in the Arabic writing at the front. In the shahada [the creed of Islam], you also keep Muhammad and Allah together. Of course this does not mean that Islam is guilty of *Shirk* in placing the two names together. As Christians we believe that Jesus the Messiah and the Holy Spirit belong inseparably together with God our Father.'

Haji Ahmed's uncertainty was almost palpable. Surely the Christian belief in God as the Trinity could not be equated with the Muslim understanding of Muhammad's relationship with Allah? 'We don't believe that Muhammad was in any way equal with God and he is not a god,' the haji declared with considerable emphasis. He then went on the offensive: 'You Christians make Jesus a god.'

Just at that moment we emerged from the woods to an open space from which we could enjoy an extensive view over the valley across the open fields, to the meandering River Lee and the trees and villages beyond. The surrounding frost-covered trees sparkled in the sunshine. In the distance the copper dome of Haileybury College's magnificent chapel reflected the bright sun. I told the haji how the German bombers had used it in the war as a navigational point on their way into London. As I went on to share how the River Lea below us had been the border between Christian Britain and pagan Britain under the Vikings for many years until around the tenth century, the haji's accusing words melted. In enjoying the beauty together, a warm sense of togetherness grew between us.

So I was able to remind him gently that actually Christians don't believe that the man Jesus became a god, but rather that God determined to come to earth and be incarnate as a human. On this topic there could be no agreement between us. 'God is *akbar* [great] and his greatness surely allows him to do whatever he wills,' I continued. The haji smiled and agreed with me concerning the unlimited greatness of Allah, but nevertheless reiterated the impossibility of reconciling the greatness of Allah with any idea of him becoming a mere human being.

As we walked across the college sports field with the beauty of the trees all around, I pointed out that the Victorians loved trees and consciously planted them so that the different shades of green formed a beautiful harmony. In this context it was natural to talk about relationships. 'Another advantage we Christians have with our knowledge of God as a Trinity is that he gives us a model for our human relationships,' I pointed out. 'The three all relate to each other in a perfect way. The Holy Spirit's aim is not to glorify himself, but to bring people to Jesus Christ and to reveal him to us. Likewise, Jesus Christ never glorifies himself, but reveals the Father and is himself the way to the Father through his death and resurrection. And the Father in turn glorifies Jesus.

Finally, at the end of this world, Jesus will lay everything at the feet of the Father, who will be all in all. So we have the perfect model in God himself of how we should relate in our families, in society, in politics and even internationally.'

'That sounds good,' Haji Ahmed agreed reluctantly, 'but actually we all know how we should relate. Every society has its cultural patterns which are good. Of course we human beings are made of clay and are weak, so sadly we don't always follow what we know to be right. But God is merciful.'

The huge brown bull in the field opposite us seemed to belie any ideas of weakness as it herded its harem of cows together. Its huge head, muscular legs and the sheer bulk of its immense body fascinated us both.

'As a Muslim you won't agree with our Christian belief in the innate sin of our human nature which we call "original sin". But we believe that humanity and therefore also our various cultures are impregnated with sin, as well as retaining something of the image of God in which we were created. So cultures give us patterns of relationships which are a mixture of good and evil. But the model we have in God is wonderfully perfect.'

'It is true that we need that model of humility and service which you speak of. But we can aim for that without having to believe in your Trinity,' the haji declared. He went on with a note of sadness in his voice, 'Here in the West, relationships are often in chaotic disorder with broken marriages, and unhappiness between siblings, as also between people at work and between neighbours. On the larger canvas of society, political and international relationships are also sadly strained. We desperately need to mend what is fractured and broken.'

As a robin perched on a branch and broke into loud song near us, I agreed with the haji. 'Yes, I'm afraid such broken relationships are causing problems now in Britain not only among our white population, but increasingly these problems seep into your Muslim young people too. The disorders of gang culture and crime, drugs and alcohol bring tragedy into all our cultures. You will appreciate therefore why as a Christian I rejoice in the perfect model to be found in God himself. And we would further stress our need of God's Spirit within us to give our people the inner power to follow God's ideal model of humble service.'

I thought to myself how beautiful life would be if we truly followed the example of the Trinity in his perfect relationships. In the Trinity the three are all different and yet absolutely one together. It is an ideal example of unity in diversity with total love and harmony.

The haji smiled. He clearly felt unwilling to pursue the question of the Trinity any further. But as we walked on between the trees with the beauty of the sun sparkling on the frost, my mind wandered to contemplate what life would be like if we all truly followed the pattern God has given us. How would it be if wives all gave themselves to seek the welfare of the husband and the husband likewise aimed to push the wife forward, to please her and to honour her? It is men who should be the ardent advocates of the rights and status of women, while women should be promoting the welfare and honour of their menfolk. I went on to muse about the relationship between workers and directors in business or industry. What would society be like if both looked for the good of the other rather than seeking benefit for themselves? In annual wage negotiations it would be the employers who would argue for more pay, better canteens and longer holidays. At the same time it would be the trade unions who would seek the good of the company and the nation. Without a sweeping movement to Christ, this seemed an impossible pipe dream.

The haji and I walked on in silence as my mind moved to God-like relationships between political parties and between nations.

'Thank you very much for all you have shared with our students and now also for our time together,' I said as Haji Ahmed and I returned to the college. I pointed out the old front door bell and the steps to help the ladies mount their horses. A student was waiting for us, ready to drive the haji down to the railway station.

'Thank you too for your openness and friendship in sharing more of your faith with me. I am always keen to understand Christianity more deeply, so I am grateful,' replied the haji with a warm smile. 'And the beauty of the college and the woods has been a real pleasure.'

It came as a relief to me that my detailed and somewhat provocative witness to biblical Christian truth had not in any way damaged the friendly relationship the haji and I had enjoyed. As I waved goodbye I could only pray that the Holy Spirit would use our relationship and the haji's increased knowledge of the truths of the gospel to bring him to faith in Jesus Christ as Saviour and God incarnate.

And I thanked God again for the beauty of All Nations and the lovely grounds which surround it. They had played an important part in allowing me to be so open in my witness. God's creation works together with his Word to testify to the full glory of God.

Reflect

How would you explain the glory of the Trinity to a Muslim?

How important do you think the visible or tangible symbols of our faith should be?

2. MUSLIM STUDENTS: SPEAKING UP

'We are going to have a series of lessons for our sixth form girls on other religions. Would you be willing to take part?' wrote a Christian religious education teacher from a north London girls' secondary school. She further explained, 'We want to invite speakers from various faiths to share why they follow their particular religion and we would like you to tell the girls why you are a Christian.'

I gathered that my lesson would be the last in the series. They would already have heard a leading representative each of Hinduism, Sikhism, Buddhism, Judaism and Islam explain what they found so attractive in their particular religion.

The school had a large sixth form, in which almost all the students were from ethnic minorities. But there were three white English students, one of whom was a committed Christian and also head girl. She enjoyed friendship and fellowship with one of the Afro-Caribbean students, a bright black girl who had been brought up in England and was well adjusted to life in London. She turned out to be a serious young lady who was determined to prove that black youngsters can work hard and succeed in life in spite of the severe social challenges they sometimes face. In her Christian faith too she had stood firm against relentless pressure from her Muslim classmates and Rastafarian boys from her own home community. She told me later she had become aware that the Christian faith was being rejected by white British people. But she had noted the moral failure both of the Rastafarians and of the surrounding white English society.

'Islam also seems to have no adequate answers to the

problems we young people face today,' she told me. 'Like so many of our black young people, Muslims so often get attracted into gang life with its potential violence. Knives and even guns cause endless trouble. So many of my Muslim friends have ended up in prison.' She went on to state her determination to be different. 'As a Christian, the Holy Spirit gives me an inner power and I want him to make me and keep me holy.'

When I had arrived at the school, the Christian head girl met me and quickly introduced me also to her friend. It seemed a God-sent opportunity to ask them how they had found the series of lessons on other faiths and what the other religious leaders had emphasized in their talks.

'Last week we had the local Muslim imam,' they informed me. 'He's from Pakistan, but spoke excellent English. He was middle-aged and passionate about the unique truth of Islam. Almost all the girls in our sixth form are also Muslim, so they keenly supported him and afterwards they really attacked us as Christians. And they were keen to persuade the few girls who have still not decided what religion they should follow, if any.'

'How did they respond to this Muslim witness?' I asked. In reply they said that the other two white English girls were not at all interested and more determined than ever to remain agnostic or even atheistic. They felt that the whole atmosphere that week just showed how religion leads to conflict and is the cause of world problems and war. 'We had to remind them that most of the wars and acts of genocide in the twentieth century were caused by atheists like Stalin and Mao, or the anti-Christian Hitler,' my new friends told me.

But the few nominally Christian black girls had come away from that day wondering whether Islam might be the answer for them. 'Islam claims to stand alongside people who have suffered from white imperialism and slavery,' they observed. The girls in question were beginning to ask themselves whether that might be true. And yet in their history lessons they had seen how slavery existed among the African tribes even before the white colonialists had come to Africa. And they knew that long before white people came to Africa, Arab slave runners had caused untold suffering among the African peoples both in West and East Africa.

'Well, what did the Muslim imam actually teach?' I asked. 'What did he choose in Islam that is specially attractive or true?'

'Of course he stressed what he called "the simple fact of the oneness of God" and strongly underlined his affirmation that Islam is God's final revelation and the only truth.'

'And then what else did he say about Islam?' I continued.

The two girls were silent for quite a while before observing, 'Now that you ask, we hadn't really thought about it, but he didn't actually talk about Islam most of the time. He mainly just attacked Christianity and tried to show that our beliefs about the Trinity are ridiculous and that the Bible is riddled with contradictions and inaccuracies. Then he seemed to assume that if we no longer followed the Christian faith, we would naturally all become Muslims.'

'When a Muslim takes that line, sometimes I tell them that if I were to abandon my faith in Jesus Christ and the Christian faith, I would probably become a Buddhist or join a synagogue,' I informed them. 'Then I ask my Muslim friend why they think it might be better to become a Muslim rather than a Buddhist or a follower of Judaism. What makes Islam so specially glorious and attractive? They seldom seem to have an answer to this.' But their description of the

Muslim imam's lesson in the previous week confirmed to me how I should start my lesson on 'Why I am a Christian'.

'I have been invited to share with you why I am a Christian,' I began. 'I don't want therefore to talk at all about other religions and why I do not follow them. My intention is to tell you some of the positive glories of the Christian faith without any attacks on other religions, their beliefs or practices. In these days in Britain we have followers of all the different faiths and it is important for good relations in society that we do not attack each other's beliefs.' It seemed right then to add, 'And in my experience non-Christians who attack the Christian faith usually distort and misunderstand what we Christians believe and practise. That always annoys me. So it is indeed best if we all follow the aim and invitation of your teacher and just talk about our own religion. I presume that the Muslim leader last week and the other speakers in previous weeks have done just that.'

Being Muslims themselves, the majority of the class sat unmoved without showing any reaction to what I said. But the few non-Muslim students smiled, for they remembered well what had happened the week before when the Muslim leader had spoken to them and pilloried the Christian faith. The two Christian girls were careful not to respond at all.

The girls listened attentively and politely with no hint of disagreement. Even the question time towards the end of the class proceeded with courtesy, although just a few aggressively propagandist questions matched the assertively black Muslim-style dress of most of the girls.

After the class a group of excited girls surrounded me and began to ply me with further questions. Some criticized the Christian faith which I had spoken about during the class, announcing with firm conviction that it was against the teaching of the Qur'an and therefore unacceptable. But the majority of the questions wanted me to declare why I was not a Muslim. 'What do you believe about Muhammad? Do you accept him as God's supreme prophet and messenger?' several asked. 'Why do you teach as if your Bible came from God when it has been altered to remove all reference to Muhammad? It's full of inaccuracies and inconsistencies,' others affirmed. 'Why don't you accept the Qur'an, God's final revelation? Look at the beauty and truth of the Qur'an; it's evidently God's miraculous revelation – with such beauty and wisdom it couldn't possibly have been written by any human being.' I remembered that Muslims believe that Muhammad was illiterate and therefore could not possibly have been the author of what they consider to be such a glorious and wise book. He was merely the scribe.

Again I stood my ground in declaring that I did not want to criticize or attack any other faith, but merely show something of the glory of the good news which we as Christians have. Again I reminded them that their teacher had invited me to the school in order to explain why I am a Christian, not to teach why I am not a follower of some other religion. 'If you want to know more about Islam, Muhammad or the Qur'an, ask your Muslim teachers. And as Muslims it's your business to face any weaknesses you may discover in your faith. Chairman Mao talked of the danger of erecting paper tigers and then shooting them down. I don't want to shoot at some incorrect version of Islam or of any other religion.'

I reminded them of what I had said in the class. What a privilege it was to share again in some detail the good news of Jesus Christ, of his sacrificial death for us to wash us clean from all sin! And what a joy to explain that we can be united with Jesus in his new resurrection life both here on earth and then eternally in the glorious presence of the Father we have come to love! Then I moved on to something which came to them as something totally new – the Holy Spirit of God. They had never before heard that Christians have God's Spirit within us to give us a new power to lead lives of holiness and to please God both personally and in our relationships.

Such opportunities to teach in religious education classes allow us to form friendly relations with young people. On such occasions one can share the gospel of Christ unthreateningly and answer Muslims' questions very personally. If we can just get on to their wavelength, young people will readily ply us with their questions and uncertainties.

Just recently my wife and I were invited to share our faith and experience in a committed Christian secondary school. Most of the students were either already Christian or unsure agnostics without any religious faith. But a few Muslims were also to be found in the midst of a very mixed student body.

'I had never heard anything much about Christianity until I came across to England and began at school here,' one overseas student explained. 'The teachers here are so different from teachers in my country,' he continued. 'They seem genuinely interested in us as people and they are so approachable too. The other guys here are generally very friendly and they don't show any sign of racial or religious prejudice. If we had a few Christian students in our Muslim school back home, they would quickly feel the pressure.' He smiled, slightly embarrassed at his confession.

As students in a foreign country, these young people had the opportunity to investigate the Christian faith without undue pressure or bias. They could observe for themselves the influence of Christianity in people's lives. Does faith in Christ make a difference in attitudes and relationships when the school is avowedly Christian? Our Muslim friends were discovering the beauty of Jesus Christ at work not only in individual lives, but also in the community life of a Christian school.

Opportunities abound among overseas students and ethnic minorities for Christians to witness to our faith in Jesus Christ in our lives, in our relationships and in our spoken testimony. This is true in secondary schools, but perhaps even more in universities. Large numbers of Muslims study in Western countries where they are more free to explore other faiths than they would be in many of their home countries. On returning home they may be significant and influential leaders in any area of society, so it is doubly important that they gain a positive impression of Christians and the Christian faith. And their conversion to Christ can have a major impact in the world of Islam. What a privilege therefore to be invited to share about Islam with Christian students in universities and also to meet with Muslim students!

'Islam and the Christian faith. Speaker: Martin Goldsmith.' The Christian Union in the university had put up their brightly coloured notices all over the campus to announce the coming meeting. The lettering was in enormous bold type and passing students could hardly fail to take note of the coming event.

The Muslim Society had also been informed of the meeting and the Christian Union secretary had personally gone to their leaders to invite them to attend. But I was unaware of all the publicity or the fact that we could expect large numbers of Muslims to be present.

Like an innocent lamb to the slaughter I made my way to the lecture hall where the evening meeting was to take place. I expected it to be a typical Christian Union gathering and it duly started in traditional fashion with the leaders gathered together for prayer. Being Jewish, I often pray with my eyes open and could therefore see what was happening in the lecture hall where the meeting was to take place.

The small band began to practise worship songs with the usual loud music. Then a few of the Christian Union members gradually arrived, some chatting among themselves while others sat quietly waiting for the meeting.

A couple of minutes before the time for the meeting to begin, a crowd of Muslims entered the hall as a group. Their leader was a young Pakistani whose deep-set, dark eyes looked out fixedly from his thin face. The aquiline nose and bushy beard beneath his white headgear fitted well with his long black robe. Behind the men came a few girls wearing complete covering to prevent the shape of their bodies being a temptation to the men. Their full Muslim dress declared to us all the girls' confident pride in their religion and underlined their identity as followers of Islam.

These Muslim students sat directly in front of me as I spoke, occupying the rows of seats near the front in the central block of the hall. Their presence felt somewhat threatening as I shared about the relationship between Islam and the Christian faith, seeking all the time to be totally fair to Muslim beliefs and to show that I was not entirely ignorant of Islamic theology and practice.

From time to time my talk was punctuated by the Muslim leader's loud exclamations of 'Allahu akbar!', God is great. Sometimes the other Muslim students joined him in these utterances. They grew particularly strong when I embarked on an exposition of the vital truth of the Trinity and the weakness of a non-trinitarian monotheism which has no relationships within the essential nature of the godhead. Such a 'simple monotheism' has no divine model for our relationships in society. Their declarations of the greatness of God became even louder when I showed how the Trinity allows us to have not only a God who is so immensely glorious and great that no mere human being can truly know or relate to him, but at the same time a God who is lovingly here with us.

After the meeting was closed the Muslim group immediately surrounded me and their leader began the attack. Although he appeared so fanatical and aggressive in his desire to preach Islam to us all, actually he turned out to be somewhat unsure of himself in his inner being. His strong words masked his personal insecurity. His slightly nervous mannerisms and jerky movements revealed his real nature, but outwardly he maintained his position as the leader of the group and the strong missionary for Islam.

'God is great! He cannot have a son!' he declared, and quoted a couple of Qur'anic verses to deny the Christian belief in Jesus as God's Son.

'As Christians we don't believe the crude idea that God took a woman and thus had Jesus as his son,' I replied somewhat defensively, but then added, 'Of course Muhammad denied that Jesus is God's Son because he lived in the midst of Arab tribes who were worshipping idols whom they called the daughters of Allah. He therefore rightly destroyed the shrines of Al-Uzza, Al-Manat and also of Allat, the supposed consort of Allah.' They all nodded their agreement as I supported Muhammad's denial of such idolatry.

Quickly I built on their momentary agreement with me, saying, 'And all of us in our various languages use the expression "son of something" but don't mean it literally or physically. For example, we can say in English that someone is a "son of a bitch". It's extremely impolite and offensive, but it clearly doesn't suggest that the person actually has a dog as physical parent. In Indonesian the digit of a finger is literally "the son of the finger"; likewise an arrow is literally "the son of a bow", the crew of a ship or plane is "the son of the ship or plane" and a key is "the son of a lock". Such expressions clearly imply a close relationship.' I went on to point out that in Islam too Muhammad is often elevated to a high level of intimacy with Allah. The spirit of Muhammad also relates closely with Allah throughout eternity. In calling Jesus God's Son, the Christian faith is also declaring the inseparable and intimate relationship of Jesus to God.

So I sought to defuse their emotive attack and show also that we Christians are not blasphemous against God's unique greatness when we affirm our belief in Jesus as God's Son. Of course I had not really explained in any meaningful way what the title 'Son of God' really means, but that would come later if these Muslim students became more open to Jesus Christ and Christianity. Their present supreme confidence in the truth of Islam and their aggressive opposition to Christianity did not encourage a careful exposition of the Old Testament use of the title 'Son of God', which must form the background to any meaningful understanding of Jesus Christ as God's Son.

In schools and universities, opportunities abound for Christians to form positive relationships with Muslim students. Public debate can go hand in hand with more personal one-on-one friendship and witness. But we would be wise to avoid acrimonious disagreement and seek rather to engage in a robust debate or dialogue where both are learning openly about the other's beliefs. Witness with our Muslim friends will challenge us to go deeper in our own biblical and theological study, learning to find adequate answers to their Muslim criticisms. We also need to avoid just defending our Christian faith against their attacks. Such a defensive approach militates against a positive testimony to the beauty and glory of the Christian good news.

Reflect

What makes the gospel of Jesus Christ 'good news' for a Muslim?

Using a concordance or Bible dictionary, explore the meaning of the title 'Son of God', firstly in the Old Testament and then in the New Testament.

3. AIRPORT ENCOUNTERS: REFLECTIONS ON PRAYER AND JIHAD

Airport terminals do not normally feature on a list of favourite locations! The one possible exception is Singapore Airport, where one can sit on a Japanese-style bridge across a pool with large brightly coloured koi fish swimming idly underneath. The pool is surrounded by a bamboo thicket with tropical bird songs issuing forth and luxurious orchids growing in the trees.

Most transit lounges cannot compete with that! They do, however, give ample opportunity to observe a fascinating array of people of every ethnic background, nation and creed.

Sometimes too one can engage in interesting conversation with other bored passengers who are only too glad to chat and be friendly. Transit lounges around the world vary significantly in what sort of passengers predominate. In the Middle East the majority will clearly be Muslim, while Chinese, Japanese and Koreans fill the Asian transit lounges. In London we may observe an amazing mix of people from all over the world.

One day in Heathrow I sat opposite a Muslim lady totally covered in black. Her sparkling eyes just managed to peep out between the layers of black material and her expensive, chic shoes revealed to us all that she belonged to a wealthy family. Next to her stood a large, fashionable handbag which further displayed her wealth and status.

After a while she carefully bent down to pick up her handbag and opened it slowly and purposely. To my surprise she took out a gold cigarette lighter and a packet of very high-quality cigarettes. What was she going to do with these? I wondered as I noted again how she was dressed. How could she possibly smoke with her face covered?

Having quietly selected a cigarette and put the packet back into her handbag, she gently lowered one part of her face covering and placed the cigarette in her mouth. With the golden lighter she then lit the cigarette, took one puff, removed the cigarette, emitted a ringed cloud of smoke and rapidly replaced the covering. After a moment or two she repeated the whole process and in this way gradually worked through the whole cigarette.

I learned two lessons as I observed this lady. Firstly, I realized that total covering does not impede normal behaviour. Despite her dress she was able to smoke and doubtless also to enjoy her food on the plane. Secondly, I observed that the simplicity of her black clothing in typical Muslim style did not prevent her from displaying her elegance and wealth. The material of her black clothing was obviously of the best quality and everyone could see her shoes and handbag with its expensive contents.

One day in Kabul, Afghanistan my wife donned full Muslim dress, being able to see out only through the small rectangle of gauze in front of her eyes. She not only realized the unbearable heat of one's breath never escaping into the atmosphere, like snuggling down with one's head under the blanket, but she also noted how limited her vision was. She could not see anything except what was directly in front of her. Anything above or below, or to either side, required a full movement of the head. Other women have told us that in a crowd they can recognize their companions only by their shoes. This of course ensures that the women are always walking submissively with heads bowed.

On another occasion I was in a long queue at Heathrow Airport, waiting to check in. Immediately in front of me stood two lively female Pakistani teenagers. They were dressed in bright T-shirts and faded old jeans and trainers. With thick Birmingham accents these girls were right at home in the English language and were using English together. Their excited chatter was heavily punctuated with much laughter. They were evidently going to visit relatives in Pakistan and were eagerly looking forward to the adventure of travelling on their own and being given VIP treatment by the family. I did just wonder whether they might find themselves pressured into an arranged marriage by their relatives in the rather remote village where their parents came from. And a question came into my mind: How would they adjust to the very traditional culture of a Pakistani rural situation?

But their talk was centred on the large copies of the Qur'an which they had in their backpacks. They were showing them to each other and laughing as they commented, 'My family will be so impressed when they see that I've brought a large Arabic Qur'an with me.' They then opened their Qur'ans and pointed at the Arabic script with considerable amusement. Unfortunately they evidently had no knowledge of the Arabic language, for they held the Qur'ans upside down!

'If you want to impress your relatives, it might be wise to hold the Qur'an the right way up,' I commented, breaking into their chatter. I helped them to turn their Qur'ans.

'Are you a Muslim?' they asked, assuming that only Muslims can know anything about Arabic.

'No, I'm a Christian. Arabic is just a language and anyone can study it as a language and thus know how to read the Qur'an in the original.'

'Do you speak Arabic?' they asked with an air of admiration.

'No,' I confessed, 'but I can read it because I've learned

the form of Malay in South Thailand which is written in Arabic script.'

'But surely Arabic is the language of Allah,' they retorted. 'After all, God wrote the Qur'an in Arabic before the creation of the world, so we thought only the followers of Allah could read his language.' I did not attempt to explain that Allah is just the Arab name for 'the Creator' and many Christians in Indonesia and other lands use the name Allah for the one Creator God. I explained that Allah is just one name for God and left it at that.[1]

It is important to realize that not all Muslims in the West have studied the Qur'an and follow Islam with zeal. Many belong strongly to their family and ethnic backgrounds, maintaining their allegiance to Islam as a mark of their identity within the cultural mix of wider society. But they may not pray regularly or follow the practices of their religion. In many ways they have become typical British young people with English as their language of communication. And theologically they may be seriously ignorant of their Islamic faith. The suicide bombers of 9/11 or 7/7 belong to a different breed from them, although they too were quite Westernized and well educated with good university training.

These two girls and I enjoyed our time together in that queue and, as we parted, I genuinely wished them the blessing of God in their visit to Pakistan.

I was reminded of these two girls later when my wife and I were passing through Dubai Airport on our way home from Pakistan. Milling crowds thronged the beautiful new airport with its palm trees and glittering decorations. A tremendous dust storm obscured the view outside and all flights were either cancelled or badly delayed. We joined a queue to change our tickets as our flight had surrendered to the swirling sand blocking all sight of the sun even in this sun-baked tropical island. The man in front of us groaned that he had already been in the queue for four hours without moving an inch, so I decided we needed to look elsewhere for help.

Wonderfully I bumped into a little knot of travellers following a smart, pink-jacketed official. He was going to open a new gate to change the tickets of people flying to London, so I asked someone to keep my place and rushed to collect Elizabeth from the previous queue. Within ten minutes we were proudly clutching our new tickets and ready to wait patiently to board our new flight in two hours' time.

Also in that queue were two young Pakistani girls in their twenties, whom we sat next to as we waited. They kindly offered us some sugared nuts, which we all munched contentedly as we began to chat and share together. There is nothing like eating together to cement a new relationship and the four of us soon felt as if we had known each other for many years. They were neatly dressed in Western clothing, but they had chosen their outfits with elegance and also modesty in mind. My wife and I quickly appreciated their choice of dress and noted its significance. It seemed to say to all who looked at them, 'We are Westernized Muslims who fit into England, but we remain sexually pure and modest in our Muslim faith.'

We did not discuss such matters as Muslim attitudes to terrorist activity or suicide bombing, but we may assume that they would surely have felt deeply uncomfortable with such behaviour. They would certainly not have wanted anything to do with the exercise of violence or attitudes of hatred.

In our friendly conversation they confessed their faith in Islam and it was evident that they followed Muslim practice with quiet assurance, but they were in no way aggressive, nor did they attempt to criticize the Christian faith when we showed that we were Christians.

'As Christians, how do you pray?' they asked us. 'And how many times a day do you pray?'

We explained to them that as Christians the method of prayer is not as important as in Islam. What is important to us is not how we pray, but rather our relationship of love for God and our faith in him and what he has done for us in Jesus Christ. 'And as Christians we don't have a set number of prayer times per day, for we enjoy an intimate relationship with God and therefore can come to him in quiet prayer at any time and anywhere.'

They also shared with us how they not only have the officially required five times of set prayer in Arabic each day, but can also pray in their own language when they have particular needs. But they admitted that they found God somewhat distant and it was hard to know for sure whether he was listening to their prayers or whether he would respond to them. 'It all depends on the will of God,' they said with a sigh. 'He can hear and answer our prayers if he so wills it, but it's hard to know for certain. But God is good and merciful, so it's probably OK.' They smiled contentedly at the thought of God's mercy. We all understood that every sura (chapter or section) in the Qur'an except one is headed with the affirmation that God is merciful, and the Qur'an emphasizes that God is merciful to those who do good. These girls were good Muslims with high moral standards, so they could feel reasonably confident of God's mercy – but deep assurance is impossible as a Muslim.

As we sat and talked, I remembered writing to Regent's Park Mosque in London, asking for some visual materials which teach about prayer in a Muslim context. We were running an annual course on Islam and wanted to show

Muslim teaching on prayer as an introduction to discussing our attitudes and reactions to it. The videos they sent us taught nothing about our relationship with God or any form of communication with the living God. Their contents consisted entirely of teaching on the details of the ritual movements required in the ablutions before prayer and then in the prayer times themselves. They answered questions such as: Do you wash the left hand and arm before the right or vice versa? Do you wash out the mouth before the top of the head? Should the fingers be exactly parallel when pointed towards Mecca? And much was said about the essential need to prostrate oneself with an absolutely straight back without any curve or bend.

So we chatted cheerfully in the transit lounge, sharing our respective faiths and enjoying our friendship. The time passed amazingly rapidly and then our flight was called. I wonder what has happened in the lives of these two lovely Muslim girls. Did our sharing together awaken a Spirit-led hunger for a better way than Islam has to offer? We could only pray.

The new Middle East airports are splendid in their modern facilities and decor with large crowds milling around the shopping areas and the various gates. But my memory slipped back to the old airports before massive oil wealth transformed everything.

In one such airport the little shopping area had been downstairs and could only be reached by means of a small moving staircase. As one was slowly transported down to the smart Middle Eastern shops, three large portraits forced themselves on the passengers' attention. In the centre of the three, the then-Emir gazed fixedly with unsmiling hard eyes above a hooked nose. 'I wouldn't like to meet him on a dark night,' I would exclaim to my wife each time we passed beneath his picture. 'If I were Emir and someone showed a picture of me looking so cruel and unpleasant, I'd have them hanged, drawn and quartered!' We wondered what character the portrait was aiming to show through that representation of the Emir's face.

On either side of the Emir's picture were two equally large portraits of his two wives. They seemed to represent a clear declaration that the Emir was in no way ashamed or embarrassed at having more than one wife. Those who support the equality of men and women may find it objectionable, but it is entirely within the rights of a man according to Islamic law.

Regal in their sumptuous attire, with obviously expensive jewellery hanging round their necks and adorning their fingers, neither of the ladies looked specially attractive. Both were middle-aged and a little overweight. Their unsmiling eyes and sagging mouths seemed to us to indicate a lack of ability to relax and enjoy their privileged lifestyle. Their facial expressions underlined the reality that wealth and privilege do not satisfy the deeper needs of the human heart. We wondered what sort of relationship they had with their husband and with each other. And how were their respective children relating together and as a family with their father and two mothers? How we wished that they could all experience something of the joy and life abundant which comes through a living relationship with God as Father through Jesus Christ!

The different airlines have their hub in their own capital city. In flying to East Asia we have had to change planes not only in Dubai, but also in Bahrain and Doha. Each of these cities has emerged in relatively recent history from their previous existence as small fishing villages surrounded by desert. Likewise, their airports have radically changed from being relatively minor into being glitteringly splendid and modern.

I remember particularly one feature of the old transit lounge in Bahrain. At the far end a large wooden relief map of Bahrain Island was displayed. It showed the whereabouts of the various oil installations, tourist sites and other major features of the island state. But what interested us was a facsimile of an old letter from Muhammad in the seventh century to the then-Emir of Bahrain. In it, Muhammad expressed his gratitude that the Emir had now agreed to accept Allah as the one God and Muhammad as his messenger. It stated that therefore Muhammad would no longer feel the necessity to send his troops down to Bahrain!

'If we had a letter like that from Jesus or from one of our esteemed leaders,' I said to my wife, 'we wouldn't want to have it on public display for everyone to read.'

'But it's unthinkable that Jesus could have ever sent a letter of that nature even if he had held political and military power in his hands,' she replied. 'And actually he chose the way of the cross in humility and suffering. He didn't seek worldly power.'

Both Jesus and Muhammad had the offer of that sort of power in their lives. In the New Testament we read how Jesus was given the opportunity of possessing 'all the kingdoms of the world and their splendour' (Matthew 4:8), but this came at the price of worshipping the devil. Does such worldly glory always involve compromised submission to Satan?

In the early days after his first prophetic revelations, Muhammad did not have many followers and he was not obviously successful in his call to be a prophet. In Mecca where he lived he did not have any influence on social or political decisions. Indeed, the people of Mecca were largely antagonistic towards him. But then he had the opportunity to move to Medina to become the leader of that city. This move to Medina, the Hijra, has become a major date in the whole development of Islamic history. The Muslim calendar is dated from the Hijra and many mosques, Muslim bookshops and other Muslim institutions are named after it.

After the Hijra Muhammad held socio-political power in his hands and this is the foundation for the holistic nature of Islam. Muhammad was not only a spiritual prophet, but also the head of state. So his authority holds sway not only in spiritual matters, but determines Muslim behaviour in every aspect of life. Shariah, the law of Islam, not only rules over one's religious life, but also over political, social, legal and economic affairs. It is all-inclusive.

'Thinking about the current Muslim situation,' my wife commented, 'it's hard to be a good Muslim with full obedience to Allah's will when Islam doesn't hold power in the state.'

'Yes,' I replied. 'Without Islamic law, Muslims will struggle to express their faith in its fullness. In contrast, Christians flourish when they live as a minority in society and even when persecution falls upon them.'

'In such circumstances,' Elizabeth responded, 'we Christians can follow the example of Jesus himself, so we know how to express our faith in practice. But we may have much more difficulty if we gain political power and have to rule.'

Jesus and the first apostles give us no clear model for the exercise of political power.

The relief map in Bahrain also raised in our minds the question of jihad which is sometimes referred to as 'holy war'. The Arabic term really signifies 'struggle'. So the question naturally arises: Who or what is the struggle directed against? The Sufis, Islam's widespread and influential mystical movement, stress that we struggle within ourselves against temptation and evil which so easily invade our personal lives.

'Jihad is in no way meant to be violent and should not involve aggression against other people,' asserted a Sufi leader to me on one occasion in the Middle East. 'It is the Muslim equivalent of your Christian longing to become more holy and to resist evil.'

It seemed somewhat bizarre to be discussing the concept of jihad or holy war in such a context. The warm evening air felt refreshing after the heat of the sub-tropical day and the gentle lapping of the Mediterranean waves formed the backdrop to my friend's explanation of jihad.

As he spoke, my mind went to Romans chapter 7 where Paul describes the battle between our worldly carnal nature and the work of the Spirit in our lives. Both Christians and Muslims know the reality that we are often aware of what is pleasing to God. In our innermost being we sincerely desire what is right. But our old sinful nature remains active within us and we cry out with Paul, 'Who will rescue me from this body of death?' (Romans 7:24). What a relief it was to be able to whisper to myself, 'As Christians we can also rejoice in the glory of the Holy Spirit of God living within us and giving us a growing victory over temptation and sin.'

As I sat back comfortably in my chair in the seaside café beside the Mediterranean, I reminded myself that Paul ends Romans 7 with the triumphant response to his despairing question, 'Thanks be to God – through Jesus Christ our Lord!' (Romans 7:25).

Looking into the serenely smiling eyes of this genial Sufi leader, I hardly dared to question him about the more violent understanding of jihad which also prevails in Islam.

It seemed ungracious even to mention such things in the presence of this avuncular middle-aged gentleman. His friendly round face and mildly overweight body with neat but comfortable Western dress belied any possibility of violence or terrorism. But I knew that in actual fact jihad is generally understood to include fighting in defence of Islam and the truth of Allah and his prophet Muhammad. So I hesitatingly broached the subject. 'Does jihad also include any counter-attack against those who threaten Islam?'

'It is a tragedy that your countries in the West have lost hold of their peace-loving Christian tradition and you have embarked on an anti-Muslim crusade,' he began, with a sad frown creasing his forehead. With my Jewish background and now with a Muslim friend I was shocked by his use of the objectionable word 'crusade' – both Jews and Muslims still have spine-chilling memories of our sufferings under the crusaders.

'Western liberal education denies the unquestionable authority of Allah and undermines the absolute truth which comes from Allah's creation of the world and his revelation of what is right. You have exported into our countries your system of inductive teaching which removes all faith in any absolute truth. The West is seeking to destroy Islam through its educational system.'

As he spoke, my mind was working overtime. To me it seemed obvious that our European educational system is not purposely aimed at destroying Islam. But at the same time I knew that it does indeed undermine faith in absolute truth, encouraging students to examine all points of view as equally valid rather than just submitting to God's revelation.

The Sufi leader became quite heated in his denunciation of what he perceived as Western aggression against Islam.

'Your media, both in television and on radio, war against our Muslim moral standards and make it impossible to live in accordance with Islamic law.'

By now his friendly smile had been replaced by a stern look of accusation. I no longer felt safe in his presence, for I was evidently associated with 'the enemy'. I began to sense that a more violent interpretation lurked strongly beneath his understanding of jihad as merely an internal struggle against evil within ourselves.

'And the West has even embarked on open wars against us Muslims – just look at what you have done in Iraq, Afghanistan, Chechnya and former Yugoslavia. And your American friends always support Israel in their aggressive denial of Palestinian rights.'

I was severely tempted to react defensively against these accusations, but held my tongue and changed the direction of our talk.

'How do you feel about the more extreme Muslims, the Islamists who follow the Egyptian Muslim Brotherhood and the even more violent thought of Maududi and Sayyid Qutb? They not only want to wage jihad against the civiliza-tions of the West, but also to destroy any Muslim societies which are not truly committed to Islamic law. Am I right in thinking that they believe that many Muslim governments and nominally Muslim adherents are blaspheming against Allah by their lives?'

My mind flashed back to Britain, knowing something of the struggle on this subject. It was reckoned in some newspapers of that time that some 35% of British Muslims praised God for the destruction brought to America in the bombings of 9/11 and would support suicide bombers in their work of jihad. Moreover, it is believed that God prom-ises Paradise to all who die while engaged in such forms of jihad. And yet the other 65% want to live in peace, feeling at home now in Britain; they are just interested in looking after their families and jobs while peacefully practising their Islamic faith.

Suddenly my friend snapped out of his heartfelt accusations, and smiled benignly with a warm word of apology. 'It is true that Islam contains within itself both understandings of jihad, the internal struggle and our defence of Allah and his messenger Muhammad.' He had returned to his normal genial self as he closed the subject by declaring, 'Of course, however, our main emphasis must remain the inner battle against sin.'

But I knew that the model of Muhammad's threat to send troops down to Bahrain to compel its people to follow the faith of Allah and his messenger has continued through the centuries down to the present day. More moderate Muslims, however, dislike this chain of Muslim violence through the centuries and earnestly desire peace and harmony in our multifaith and multi-ethnic societies. Will they be able to gain the upper hand within the community of Islam worldwide? Much depends on the answer to this question.

Reflect

How would you explain your Christian practice of prayer to a Muslim friend?

How should we live as Christians when we are an unpopular or persecuted minority?

4. ON THE WAITING LIST FOR JESUS: WHEN CULTURES MERGE

My hostess welcomed us in from the damp cold of a Scottish November evening. The warmth in her middle-aged eyes embraced us and we immediately felt comfortably at home. She ushered us gently into her little front room where a bright wood fire held our attention; its flames danced along a handsome log and reached up towards the chimney. The slightly worn, old-fashioned furniture demonstrated that this was not a wealthy home where new and up-to-date acquisitions could prevent their occupants from sinking snugly into them. We relaxed at the end of a busy day and enjoyed the hot chocolate, home-made scones and a biscuit.

But we were not alone as guests. Already relaxing in the love of that Christian home sat a young lady, who immediately stood up to greet us and introduce herself. A faint foreign accent betrayed her otherwise excellent English and her white skin. Jet-black hair and quietly dignified dark eyes with a prominent Roman nose suggested to us her West Asian background. It seemed natural to ask her where she came from and without hesitation she told us that she was from Iran. Unlike some Iranian refugees, she appeared unafraid of people knowing who she was and where she came from.

'Are you a Christian?' we asked after some further conversation.

To our considerable surprise she replied, 'No, not yet. I am still a Muslim.' Her eyes shone with a quiet dignity and she smiled patiently as she added, 'I am on the waiting list to become a Christian.'

We did not like to admit that even after fifty years in Christian ministry we had never before heard such a testimony. But her maturity and friendly self-confidence encouraged us to repeat her words quietly and enquiringly: 'On the waiting list?'

Without any embarrassment she explained, 'My church has a rule that no-one should become a Christian until they have done the Alpha Course, and I was too late in applying to find a space on the most recent course.'

We noticed the words 'my church' and realized that she was already participating in the life of a Christian church, despite the fact that she affirmed that she was still a Muslim. With its emphasis on externalism, Islam considers its followers to be still Muslim until they receive the outward sign of entry into another religion and openly renounce their Muslim faith. So until our friend could be baptized as a Christian, with this visible outward sign of her Christian faith, she was still reckoned to be Muslim.

With a gentle smile our Iranian friend continued her explanation. 'You see, our church has a further rule that no Alpha Course should have more than forty Muslims in the group and the last course was already full when I applied.' She continued with happy confidence, 'But I am right towards the top of the waiting list for the next course and I am determined to become a Christian at the end of it.'

We were not surprised to hear that her Iranian church was growing apace, for she explained to us that generally at the end of each course all the Muslims attending would become believers in Jesus as their Lord and Saviour. They would then be baptized and join the Christian church. And so the church would grow by some forty new members after each Alpha Course. We rejoiced at how the Holy Spirit was using this course so wonderfully not only among our fellow de-Christianized British, but also with ethnic minority people who may come from a background of other faiths.

There are several other courses which introduce enquirers to Jesus Christ and the Christian faith, but we could see the fruit that comes from the fact that the Alpha Course is based in much prayer. It also encourages open discussion in groups, which allows Muslim-background enquirers to voice their difficulties and hear a clear and relevant Christian answer without hostile disagreement. But perhaps what specially appeals to ethnic minority participants is the food beforehand. In so many cultures, as in the Bible, eating and drinking together has deep significance and binds people together in a personal relationship which opens the door for free discussion. It forms the right unthreatening atmosphere in which to find a new faith in Jesus Christ.

We began to ask more about our friend's Iranian church. She told us about its rapid growth and the fellowship they all enjoyed together there. 'We are of course all Iranian, facing the same problems and difficulties,' she told us. 'We have all had to flee from the oppressive Islamic revolution in Iran. It is so dictatorial – if you don't toe the line, you face tremendous danger and may well be killed or at least imprisoned.' A steely glint hardened her eyes and replaced the gentle smile which had previously encouraged an easy friendliness between us. 'They are so ruthless and cold-hearted,' she declared and her lips set firmly. 'If that is what Islam means when it is practised without restraint and in its fullest form, you can keep it!'

Her bitter declaration and the personal experiences which evidently lay behind her words contrasted markedly with the loving atmosphere of the home in which we were sitting. Here the welcoming love of Christ enfolded us in its comfort. The heat and beauty of the wood fire seemed only to reinforce the reality of Christian love and peace. In such a home there was total freedom to share openly and talk without fear or restraint. My wife and I had never met either our kind hostess or this Iranian lady before, but already within a very short space of time we felt a loving oneness together. We realized yet again the beauty of fellowship in the love of Jesus which can bind together people of very different backgrounds. I am Jewish, our hostess was Scottish, our friend was from an Iranian Muslim background and my wife is English but also partly Norwegian and American. But in Jesus Christ we felt our unity and the home we were in symbolized that love and welcome which Jesus offers us all.

But in my mind there were also some niggling little questions. This Iranian church uses only Farsi in its meetings, so cannot receive people of other backgrounds. Inevitably this must narrow it down into something of a ghetto-like existence, in which it is separated from the masses of English-speaking people among whom the church's followers live and work. Will that narrowness make the church too exclusive in its outlook? How will it learn from other Christians who do not speak Farsi and are not from Iran? What witness will this church have among the surrounding Scottish population or even among other ethnic minorities in the city? What will this church contribute to the life and witness of the wider church in Britain? Will it be able also to encourage its members to lift up their eyes and see the need for mission among all peoples all over the world?

I knew from experience of Jewish messianic fellowships and from my relationship with British Chinese churches that there are very real dangers in such ethnic churches. But of course there are also big advantages which we must not ignore.

It is so heart-warming to enjoy fellowship with people of one's own cultural background. I know the joy of this when meeting together with other Jewish believers in such messianic fellowships or in the board meetings of 'Jews for Jesus'. There is a freedom to communicate in your own cultural way, laughing together with others who share your sense of humour. But more important still is the fact that the teaching will be adapted to the particular needs and situations faced by their members. Thus Iranians coming from the background of the Islamic revolution have emotional and security questions which are quite different from those of the average British church member. And new Christians from a Muslim background will also have their own particular questions and issues. These need to be addressed by the teaching and preaching of the church, if young believers are to be truly brought into maturity as followers of Christ. A purely Iranian church can definitely cater for such needs among their own people.

Perhaps the best solution would be to have ethnic churches which relate closely to other churches in their neighbourhood and engage in evangelism, Bible teaching and other activities together. An alternative might be that the ethnic church could become like a cell group in a larger multinational church, with autonomy to run its cell group in ways suited to its people's background and culture. In this way the ethnic church would also have the more mature discipline, biblical teaching and godly tradition of the older and larger church. But the leadership of the mother church would have strictly to refrain from imposing the shackles of their tradition in worship and biblical or theological understanding on the ethnic fellowship. Together they would seek to glorify the Father, Jesus Christ and the Holy Spirit under the authority of God's Word, the Bible.

'We are praising the Lord in our church because last month we had three Muslims confessing their faith in Christ through baptism.' How often I have heard such words as I minister in a wide variety of churches not only in Britain, but also in other countries. 'Were they from Iran?' I often ask innocently. Again and again the Christian I am talking with is very surprised. 'Actually, yes! They were from Iran. How did you know?'

In his sovereign lordship over the movements of the world and all peoples, God seems at different times of history to cause his church to grow significantly among different peoples. In the last thirty years there has been enormous political and religious upheaval in Iran and this may have been God's way of triggering a new disillusionment with Islam and therefore an openness to the gospel. This may be particularly true of refugees from Iran who have suffered severely at the hands of their Muslim rulers, but have found a haven in the traditionally Christian nations.

In our day we are seeing growing numbers of Muslims all around the world coming to a knowledge of Jesus Christ, but this is taking place more among some peoples than others. It is important for our witness among ethnic minorities in our own country that we realize that Iranian Muslims may very well be open to the message of the gospel. On the other hand, Somali refugees tend to hold together in strong social units and are at present firmly resistant to the good news of Jesus Christ. People from other national backgrounds will include some who are open, but they may not quite compare in openness with the Iranians in our midst.

In former times we used to think that Muslims were all strongly opposed to the gospel and unwilling to consider the possibility of faith in Jesus Christ as our Lord and Saviour, but this is no longer true. Many Muslims are now very open to the message of Christ. This is the sovereign work of the Holy Spirit and we rejoice. Let us enter through the open doors God is giving us for witness among our ethnic minority neighbours.

There was one particular incident of worship at a conference centre that I remembered vividly as we talked with our Iranian friend in Scotland. Was the worship in her Iranian church in some way like the recent conference I had attended? How far did the Muslim background of her church members influence their worship together?

The conference centre at High Leigh in Hertfordshire had buzzed with animated interaction. Christian leaders from around the world had come together for a few days to discuss the practice of mission among Muslims. Various papers were read and debated, discussion groups were constantly too short and we all felt that we had only scratched the surface of the various topics. But perhaps the heart of the conference lay in our times of coffee and meals when we could meet one another individually, share together informally and really learn from each other.

On one particular day, feelings ran high. 'This Muslim-style worship is unbiblical rubbish, a compromise of true Christian faith. If people want to remain Muslim, don't let them pretend to be followers of Jesus Christ!' A white South African friend of mine was clearly angry and his loud voice resounded in the conference centre hall. In the middle of our worship time in the conference, he had stood up and stalked out of the room in protest.

In sharp contrast a different response could be heard. 'That was wonderful,' beamed a vivacious Nigerian mission leader, Ibrahim, with an expansive, white-toothed smile. 'Never before have I experienced such relevant worship. It made the glory of God so real and evident in our midst.

I have always in the past had difficulty with our Christian worship. It is so Western in its forms and it is hard to realize the splendour of Christ in such worship.' Ibrahim had been a strongly religious Muslim, strictly practising his faith. He had prayed regularly five times a day and had been in the mosque at least once a day, and not just for the midday Friday prayers. At Ramadan no food or drink of any sort ever passed beyond his throat and he had been several times to Mecca on the pilgrimage. Having a Jewish culture myself, I knew just what he meant and how he felt, for I too sometimes find Western Christian worship culturally alien.

So what had that evening's worship been like? The scene was set by removing all chairs and having us sit cross-legged on the floor with the men on one side and the women on the other. Already some of the more conservative delegates at the conference were beginning to feel uncomfortable. 'Is this some sort of gimmick?' they asked each other. 'What's wrong with having chairs? Why do we have to sit in this uncomfortable way? And it's not just for five minutes!'

Their sense of unease had already been incited by us all being asked to wash our hands and faces in water as we entered the hall. This symbolic act underlined the fact that we can only enter the presence of the all-holy God with clean hands and hearts. We were all aware that just washing hands and faces was a little different from the Muslim washings before entering the mosque, but the symbolism seemed appropriate and biblical. Nevertheless, the more conservative members felt it was like the Roman Catholic practice of having holy water at the entrance of the church. So they already felt uncomfortable even before they entered the hall and had to sit on the floor. But people from other cultures rejoiced in the significance of this symbolic act.

The worship leader had converted from a Middle

Eastern Muslim background and he began to explain to us the outward forms of salat, Muslim mosque worship. Then he guided us in how we could delete all reference to Muhammad and the Qur'an, substituting Jesus and biblical content. 'In our worship we shall all face Jerusalem like Daniel did when he was praying,' he told us and then added, 'I do realize that the direction of Jerusalem is rather similar to the qibla [the direction of Mecca].' He smiled broadly. 'But we won't let that British problem disturb us.'

The worship proceeded along the lines of the Muslim salat, though the words had been radically altered to exalt Jesus Christ and to accord with biblical revelation. But the outward movements remained as in the salat. So at one stage we all had our index fingers pointing towards Jerusalem and exactly parallel with each other. When we prostrated ourselves before the Lord we were instructed to keep our backs from bending at all, for it is important in the salat to keep the back utterly straight. At the right time too we looked over our shoulders at the people standing next to us to demonstrate our unity in Jesus Christ and to confirm that no gap was left between the people of God, into which an evil spirit might slip unnoticed!

Do such amended forms of worship constitute a compromise of the true faith of Jesus Christ according to the Bible? Are they just a trick to entice Muslims into the church, but with the inevitable result that Islam and Christianity are mixed together in an unholy muddle? Or is it biblically acceptable to fit our worship forms to the local context, in order that there may be no stumbling block to faith and discipleship except the scandal of the cross and resurrection of Jesus? Do such forms of worship help Muslims to become Christian more easily? Or do they form a bridge whereby it becomes easy for Muslim-background believers to forsake their Christian faith and slip back into Islam?

As a Jewish Christian myself such questions are of vital significance, for my people too are struggling to find what forms of Christian worship and prayer are suited to our Jewish background. We know that Western forms of worship do not fit our Jewish context, where the centre of our religion lies in the home rather than the religious building. Joyful celebration is based around a festive meal together, full of colour and light. But still we remain unsure as to how far we can go with Jewish forms without losing the heart of our Christian faith. Such questions turned in my mind after our encounter with our Iranian friend.

I also knew something of the problem of the church fitting in with the cultural and ethnic background of the first generation of an immigrant community. That first generation usually huddles together in a ghetto for security and companionship.

What a privilege it was to get to know Aziz, one such first-generation member. His short frame sagged in outsize trousers and an old shirt, but his wrinkled face smiled shyly when he was with people he trusted. Coming in middle age to England from Pakistan, he soon found himself crowded into a back-to-back urban English house with various cousins and second cousins plus their families. He could make himself understood in his somewhat inadequate English, but his wife knew no English at all. They were already too old to adapt to life in England, feeling more at home shopping in the local Pakistani food store. In that area of the city he was surrounded by crowds of other Pakistanis, so it was rare that he needed to switch from his native Urdu into English. In his uncertainty when faced with problems like filling out social security forms or having to go to a doctor, he was grateful for local Christians' help. As a result he felt very positive about the Christian faith, although it never entered his mind that he would ever join such a foreign religion. He was born a Muslim and he would surely remain one until his dying day, he felt. Any Christian worship service would have seemed totally strange to him.

Second-generation immigrants, however, will gain their education in the new country. They will be surrounded by local friends and so will most probably speak English like a native. They also know how to fit in with local cultural forms, behaving in a British way quite naturally. So they grow up with two cultures, British as well as that of their parents. If they do not experience racial prejudice and discrimination, they will continue happily with their local friends. For example, my own mother felt completely at home in Britain and found herself reacting as a late teenager against the narrow Jewish community of her parents. Going to an English school, she broke out into the wider local groupings around her, got baptized and found a job in the League of Nations in Geneva.

The third generation may become even more assimilated into the host community and culture than their parents, but on the other hand they may find their identity in radical forms of their faith. So it is in Europe today that extremist Islamists often stem from the apparently very Western third generation.

This enormous generation gap in outlook can cause considerable heartache to parents and to the older generation. As local Christians, therefore, we may play a significant role in helping such people to understand what is happening with their children and the younger generation. Young people of the second and third generations of immigrant communities may then blend in with the host nation and may also be very open to the Christian faith.

On the other hand, it is a sad reality that many third-generation immigrants will experience racial prejudice and discrimination. They may run a mile from local contacts, not believing that English people can ever be genuine and friendly. In bitterness they may return to their Islamic roots – not from insecurity like their parents, but rather because they may be consumed with real hatred of Britain and their white English compatriots. Fanatical extremism breeds angrily among such people, even if outwardly they are succeeding in their education and professional life. Violent hatred is certainly not the reserve of the poor and unemployed, as seen with the attempted bombing of Glasgow Airport by a group of highly educated and successful doctors.

Our Iranian friend's church was ideally suited to the first generation of refugees from Iran, but I was haunted by the question: Will her church be adequately flexible to adapt to the changes in the second and third generations?

Reflect

Why do you suppose some peoples are more open to the gospel than others? How does the Holy Spirit work in preparing people for the message of Jesus Christ?

How far do you think our worship should be adapted to the cultures of different generations and peoples? Try to think through what forms of worship might suit Muslim converts to Christ.

5. SULEIMAN AND THE JINN: FOLK ISLAM AND EVIL SPIRITS

'Is it really true that you can deal with the jinn and help someone who is having trouble with such spirits?' Suleiman almost whispered to me after he had talked nervously for quite a long time about other things. Suleiman and I had met before and chatted together about all sorts of subjects. In the midst of our talking together I had previously mentioned quite casually that as Christians we have power over all spirits in the name of Jesus the Messiah. The topic of evil spirits touches a raw nerve among many Muslims because occult practices remain common in their community. Many people are troubled by demonic attacks in their personal lives and in their homes. But when I had broached the topic earlier, Suleiman had not picked it up. However, he had evidently not forgotten it. Now he came for help.

Coming from a conservative Pakistani community in Bradford, Suleiman wore the traditional flowing brown outfit with Muslim headgear and sandals. His face was clean-shaven with no hint of a beard, showing that he was not by any means an Islamist extremist in the practice of his faith. His long thin fingers tapped nervously on the table by his side, his head hung downwards with his eyes gazing unseeingly at the floor. Normally he carried his position as a mature married man in his early thirties with quiet, dignified confidence, but today he was different. He was evidently embarrassed to approach me on the subject of the jinn, although in previous visits together he had been amicable, with a gentle smile enlivening his dark eyes. But now his eyes were troubled, lacking their customary sparkle.

'I have no power over spirits in myself,' I declared with my right hand held to my heart in the Muslim sign of humility and respect, 'but I believe that Jesus the Messiah has such power and can help us still today. In his lifetime here on earth 2,000 years ago, he showed that he can cast out evil spirits and deliver people from the spirits' grasp. And now in our time he still works miracles through his followers.'

Suleiman's head began to lift and his eyes moved from looking at the floor. He still did not have the confidence to look directly at my face and thus his eyes still did not meet mine, but hope was beginning to penetrate the darkness of his problems. Could this foreign friend who was not even a Muslim actually help him? Would a Christian be able to deal with his problem when all Muslim means had failed? Such thoughts were clearly going through his mind, but he certainly did not want to express them openly.

'Are you or your family being troubled by a jinn?' I asked with some hesitation, not wanting to intrude on his private problems before he was ready to share them with me. But it seemed only kind to help him express the very reason why he had come to visit me that morning. Happily the Christian friends with whom I was staying had gone out and we were alone together, so no-one else needed to be taken into consideration as he revealed the burden he was carrying.

'Yes. I was wondering whether perhaps you might be able to help my wife and me. We are facing a difficulty and cannot find a way out.' He then told me how he had been to the Muslim sheikh, who had not been able to help him in any way. He had recommended prayer and strict obedience to Allah's commands concerning fasting and the payment of zakat. But Suleiman's strict adherence to Islam had not provided a way out of his difficulties. So he had then called on the local Muslim shaman (spirit man), who had gone into a trance and performed certain dances, calling out various Qur'anic texts and issuing commands as to what Suleiman and his wife should do. The shaman had demanded considerable money in payment for his ministry. But nevertheless their problem persisted.

Suleiman had still not dared to give voice to what exactly his problem was. So I felt the need to prompt him again and encourage him to put it into words. 'Would you like to tell me what is happening with yourself and your wife?' I asked.

At first his reply came with considerable uncertainty and hesitation. Then the words began to tumble out as he gained confidence.

'I know that sometimes a jinn can be friendly and helpful to us, but this one is evil and we are frightened,' he told me.

In Islamic belief the devil is totally evil and he has messengers who are called Shaitan. This is the same word as the biblical term 'Satan' and these beings are fundamentally evil, although they can on rare occasions do what is good. Below them come the jinn who are more like the traditional British 'imp': sometimes good and helpful, but unreliable and often bringing harm to people. Thus in the Muslim story of Aladdin the 'genie' or jinn is a servant to help any who are able to call upon him. But usually a jinn is dangerous and will bring misfortune on those with whom it crosses paths.

So I wondered what Suleiman's experience would have been. And then would come the more serious question of how the Lord would want the matter dealt with.

'At night we close our windows and draw the curtains before we go to sleep,' he started. I almost felt I knew the rest of the story before he continued, for I had heard similar accounts from other British Muslims on several occasions.

The devil seems to have certain fixed ways of working which he repeats with different people.

'Suddenly in the middle of the night when we are deeply asleep, the curtains suddenly get pulled open with such a noise that it wakes us up.' Then he added a vivid description of how on other occasions in the middle of the night, the taps in their bedroom washbasin would suddenly be turned on full, so that the water would gush out in a torrent and wake them up.

Both the curtains opening and the turning on of the taps occurred from time to time, not just once. It was clear that these happenings were bringing real fear into the lives of Suleiman and his wife. As Christians we know that 'perfect love drives out fear' (1 John 4:18), so fear-inducing happenings directly contravene the will of God.

These events were clearly supernatural, for there could be no ordinary explanation for the taps coming on in this fashion when everyone was asleep. Likewise Suleiman assured me that their windows were double glazed and there could be no wind or draught seeping through to blow the curtains open. No, there could only be a spiritual explanation. So, if they did not come from God, they could only be satanic in origin. An evil spirit was evidently at work.

'God can drive out the evil spirit if we pray accordingly in the great name of Jesus,' I assured Suleiman. But I went on to tell him of the danger of driving out an evil spirit without at the same time filling one's life with the Spirit of Jesus the Messiah. Jesus warned the Pharisees and teachers of the Law of this danger. When an evil spirit is driven out, he said, it will return with seven even worse spirits unless it is replaced by the Spirit of Jesus himself, the one who is greater than Jonah or Solomon (Matthew 12:38–45). It was vitally important to encourage Suleiman to turn in faith to Jesus and fill his life with his saving grace, for otherwise 'the final condition of that man is worse than the first' (Matthew 12:45).

Suleiman turned sadly away, for he was not yet ready to believe in Jesus and follow him as his Lord and Saviour. He never came again to visit and talk with me. It often happens that when someone definitely rejects Jesus, they may also break their relationship with the messenger who was bringing the good news of Jesus to them. The person and their witness go hand in hand.

The devil not only uses curtains and taps to bring fear and thus to bind people to himself. Many Muslims tell of one corner in their front room being deadly cold while the rest of the room is nicely warm. There seems to be no natural reason for this phenomenon either and again it brings real fear into the lives of those who experience it. No double-glazed windows or central heating can prevent it.

I have observed too that the cold corner of the room is unnatural in another way. A clear line divides the cold part of the room from the other parts. There is no gradual warming of the air as one progresses from that corner into the rest of the room. Suddenly in a single step one moves from icy coldness into normal warmth.

It is a mystery why Satan uses these particular phenomena to instil fear into those whom he wants to oppress. But the consequences are very clear. The Muslims involved are bound by a very real fear and Satan rules without resistance in their lives. There can be no doubt that occult practices in folk Islam have spiritual power over those who in some way have strayed into that arena.

The New Testament reality of Jesus' authority over all evil powers is vitally important in dealing with these circumstances. As people come to faith in him, he can deliver them from all spiritual oppression. In such contexts we need to rediscover the old Reformation baptism liturgies in which the new believer is pointedly asked whether they will turn from Satan and all his works. Only then are they asked whether they will follow Christ in righteousness. In conversion and baptism we turn not only from sin, but also from Satan himself with all his evil spirits. They stand in direct opposition to the Lord and are the cause of sin. So the early church's confession of faith was that 'Jesus is Lord' – no longer may Satan or his demonic messengers hold sway in our lives.

Experience with the demonic work of evil spirits came as a shock to me when I first went to work in Asia. Having come to Christ and grown in my Christian life within the context of conservative evangelical teaching, I had never witnessed such activity of Satan. And in my biblical and theological studies it would have been quite unacceptable to talk or write about demons or evil spirits, although the Gospels frequently refer to them. At that time Satan did not commonly show his hand in overt demonic activity and in theological studies it was definitely considered unacademic to accept the stories of demon possession literally.

So my encounter in Singapore with Hindu fire-walking posed questions which lay right outside my mission preparation. Standing close to the long pit, I felt the blazing heat of the red-hot coals across which the Hindu devotees quietly walked with bare feet. I could not doubt the reality of the burning heat and it was evident that the men suffered no injury to their feet as they walked or ran through the pit of coals. It could not be explained naturally and the fearful reality of the power of Satan began to break into my thinking. Then came the question of how we as Christian workers should relate to such demonic power and activity.

In Singapore I also witnessed Hindu men carrying heavy

idols on wooden platforms attached to their bodies with iron hooks. With skewers through their cheeks and lips, they danced hypnotically through the streets, bearing the swaying idol on its platform. Finally they danced to the rhythmic clapping of the crowds around the outer precincts of the temple. Before the altar of the deity, the priest took down the image of the god and pulled out the skewers and the hooks, daubing the bodies with holy ash. The Hindu devotees then quietly walked away, going outside the temple and buying a cold drink to refresh themselves after the exhausting exercise of dancing in the heat. But their bodies showed no sign of damage and they themselves returned unperturbed to normal life!

Later in South Thailand I met with Muslim shamans (spirit men) who also had very definite spiritual powers, allowing them to perform supernatural miracles.[1] One of these shamans revolved his head at such speed that his long hair came loose and sped round and round like a propeller or electric fan. It spun at such a speed that one could not tell exactly where the hair was at any given moment.

The other shaman would go out to sea with groups of fishermen, listen for the sound of fish with his head in the water and then direct the boats on where to go to catch the fish. He could hear fish at a distance of several miles and know exactly what sort of fish they were, what direction they were moving in and how fast. We know that fish do indeed make a noise and with scientific equipment one can pick up the call of whales, but it is surely impossible to hear the sound of smaller fish with the naked ear at several miles' distance. There can be little doubt that both these shamans were right in their claim that these miracles were performed through the power of the spirits.

Gradually through such experiences I began to learn

the reality of evil spirits and how to deal with them in my mission ministry. I learned to include in my evangelistic work the glory of Jesus' promise to deliver his people from all satanic attack. As people turned to Jesus for salvation, they needed to repent of all connections with evil spirits or demonic worship. Charms and other things associated with such idolatry or evil spirit activity had to be destroyed and all personal links with evil spirits specifically abjured. If the individual had been dedicated to a particular spirit or deity in their youth, all such connections must be cut off as the new believer invited Jesus to fill their life as their Lord and their Saviour.

So it was that I felt confident to let it be known among Muslims in Bradford at that time that in the name of Jesus they could be delivered from the attacks of any jinn or evil spirit. The love of Jesus could replace the fear which the devil delights in causing in the lives of people who are under his sway. Some Muslims today even in the West are discovering the glory of the gospel, the good news of Jesus who saves us from the power of Satan and evil spirits as well as from the guilt and consequences of sin.

Both in the Old and the New Testaments, God often reveals himself and his purposes by means of visions or dreams. For example, the dreams which Joseph interpreted when he was in prison in Egypt are well known. The apostle Paul's meeting with the resurrected Jesus on the road to Damascus converted him from a zealous persecutor of Christians to a key Christian leader who pioneered the preaching of the gospel beyond his own Jewish circles into the Gentile world. Later he was called to preach the gospel in Macedonia too by means of a vision. Angelic visitations with specific messages from God prepared the way for the birth of Jesus, and the New Testament concludes with the glorious vision which John received from heaven in the book of Revelation. It is by no means a novelty that God often speaks to Muslims through visions or dreams. With their religious and cultural background, they find no difficulty in receiving God's message by such means.

In talking with Muslim-background believers in many different countries around the world, I have frequently heard testimonies of people whose conversion started with a dream or vision. Knowing that God often fits his means of revealing himself to our cultural expectations, I advise Christian workers among Muslims to let it be known not only that they can deliver others from evil spirits, but also that they can interpret dreams and visions. And we need to pray particularly that the Lord in his wonderful grace will give dreams or visions to our Muslim friends to convince them of the reality of Jesus the Messiah and his saving work for them.

'But I have never in my life interpreted a dream,' some Christians respond with embarrassment. 'I would be completely flummoxed if anyone came to me with their dream in the hope that I might be able to help.'

'Don't worry!' I reassure such people. 'If God is wanting to reveal something, he will make it clear. And if you don't understand the significance of the dream, be honest and say so. Then you can pray with the person and ask God to give the dream again, but in a way which makes the meaning obvious. At least, in this way you will have an ongoing relationship with your Muslim contact and within a very personal context.'

A Muslim lady in North Africa had the same dream again and again. She was sure that it was significant, but had no idea what it could mean. In her dream she saw a very attractive road which was easy to walk along, but she noticed that it led somewhere frighteningly awful. Then she also saw a second road which went steeply uphill and was difficult to climb because of many potholes. But this second road led to somewhere beautiful.

'I so want to get on to that second road,' she informed her Christian friend. 'But to do so, you have to go through a gateway which has a dark power over it.' With real fear she added, trembling, 'Whenever I try to get through the gateway, the dark power fights me. This leads to such a fearful struggle that I wake up bathed in perspiration and never succeed in getting through to the road.'

When she was shown the words of Jesus concerning the two ways (Matthew 7:13–14), she exclaimed, 'How did the author of that book know my dream?' She assumed that her dream came first, that the author of the Bible had somehow learned the content of her dream! Her friend assured her that the one who gave her the dream was also the one who inspired the Bible – and the Bible was written long before her dream.

In East Malaysia a Muslim soldier on night-time guard duty saw a vision of a brilliant cross stretching from end to end of the night sky. He knew that the cross was a Christian symbol, so went into his barracks to wake up a Christian friend. He felt the vision was surely for the Christian, not for him as a Muslim.

When the Christian soldier saw the cross in the sky, he told his friend, 'God gave this vision to you, not to me. God obviously wants to speak to you particularly. He wants you to believe in Jesus who died on the cross for you.'

In neither of the above stories do you need any special gift of interpretation. The meaning is in both cases very obvious to anyone with even a basic knowledge of the Bible. In our relationship with Muslims and in our witness among them, we should remain strongly aware of the possibility of God speaking to them through a dream or vision. Such supernatural messages from God give Muslim converts added confidence and courage when they face fierce opposition and even persecution for their faith. They need that definite proof that God is powerful and will work on their behalf when trouble comes.

Reflect

What experience, if any, have you had of occult or demonic activities? How far does this influence your understanding of the New Testament stories about evil spirits?

Explore the role of dreams and visions in the New Testament.

6. THE POLYGAMOUS SHEIKH: WHAT ABOUT OTHER FAITHS?

Spicy food! Superb curries! Lots of Asian rice! The warm hospitality and fellowship of my Pakistani Christian hosts were in marked contrast with the damp drizzling cold outside in a run-down area of a northern British city. The hedges had forsaken all attempts to give colour as their dark grey-green leaves seemed to sag under the weight of the November clouds. Litter blew around in the harsh wind, and the overcrowded houses spilled out their Asian occupants without enthusiasm. The whole area seemed to shiver in the cold of approaching winter.

And yet in the midst of such desolation, neighbours gave a friendly greeting to one another. Little knots of men stood stoically outside the local corner shop as they talked together. People struggled to maintain the warmth of their traditional Asian climate and culture. Although most of the women were totally covered in black and the men still kept to their brown outfits, some younger girls defiantly and courageously braved the pressures of the dull surrounding gloom and their parents' Somali and Pakistani backgrounds, daring to appear in bright Western clothes. Inside the local library, some of the ladies reflected the welcoming lights overhead with their brightly coloured Indian saris.

What a racial mix in such a small area of the city! The majority followed the faith of Islam, but a few were Hindu or Christian. Serving the Christians and seeking to witness among the Muslims, my Pakistani hosts, Aziz and his wife, stood out. They had been my students some years previously and it was a privilege and pleasure to watch them putting into practice what they had learned.

Many of the local Muslims thought that, as a Christian, Aziz would have more acceptance with the Home Office. As a result, he received a steady stream of visitors who asked him to support their claim for asylum in Britain. Some suggested that he could claim that they were married to a British citizen, although this was not the case. A whole variety of possible reasons were put forward as to why the authorities should look favourably on their applications. Most of these suggestions were clearly untrue, but that did not seem to worry Aziz' visitors.

'I'm so sorry, but I'm afraid I cannot help you,' Aziz would apologize. 'I have no pull on the Home Office and actually they don't favour Christians at all. Indeed, they often seem opposed to anyone who claims to be Christian.' When it was appropriate he would also explain, 'As a Christian I also don't believe in supporting claims which are based on a lie.' Aziz was careful to keep right out of any political involvement in helping people with their residence or citizenship applications. But despite his continual refusal to get caught up in these, people still hoped that he would make an exception just for them, so visitors continued to arrive at his door.

While I was staying with Aziz and his wife, we had another visitor. Sheikh Omar was originally from Egypt and was clearly the leader for the whole local Muslim community. In this role he sought to bring the various ethnic groups together within the orbit of the local mosque. This proved quite difficult, for the Somalis felt themselves to be very different from the Pakistanis and Bangladeshis. The Somalis kept very much to themselves within their own community. Other Muslims looked down on them as unreliable and dishonest. 'Never trust anything a Somali says,' one Pakistani said to me. 'They don't know what truth is.'

Sheikh Omar walked with upright pride and confidence in his Muslim attire. He was tall for an Egyptian and stood out in the local crowds. His grey-brown face was thin, tapering into a small pointed beard. His eyes were sharp above his aquiline nose. His mouth bent downwards at either end like in cartoon pictures of unhappy people. I wondered whether indeed discontent reigned in his life in spite of his role as a leading teacher of Islam.

'Have you seen my teaching course which I use to instruct the people of Islam in this area?' he asked me with unconcealed pride in the course he had written. When I confessed that I did not know of his course, he quickly informed me, 'As a religious leader you would be interested. I will bring a copy round and I would be glad of any comments you may have concerning its contents.'

Later that afternoon he came round for another brief visit and handed me a copy of his teaching course. When he had left, I read it through. I was shocked by the many blatant errors of fact concerning both Judaism and Christianity. It also made scathing attacks on both faiths, often based on misunderstandings and misrepresentations of what they believe.

'Aziz, I dare not tell the sheikh what I feel about his beloved course of which he's so proud. If I listed the many mistakes it would just cause a break in relationships. He probably wouldn't accept my criticism and he would find it embarrassing within his community to have to confess that his teaching had been riddled with errors. What should I do?' Aziz duly gave me his advice.

When we visited Sheikh Omar one day I duly thanked him for graciously allowing me to see the course. 'I think you might do well to ask a leader from the Jewish synagogue to correct any misunderstandings of Jewish thought and worship. There are a few things about Judaism in your course which may not be quite accurate,' I suggested with some hesitation. 'And I personally feel some of your ideas about what we as Christians believe are also not quite accurate. I'm only here for a relatively short time, so cannot go through it in detail with you, but perhaps Aziz could discuss the various points with you and then the two of you could work together on the course.' Aziz had felt that this would give him the opportunity of discussing the Christian gospel with the sheikh.

There was something important in common between the sheikh's course and Aziz' many visitors wanting him to help them with immigration problems. Neither seemed to have much regard for truth. For many Muslims it is more important to avoid shame than to speak truth or act honestly. These matters further reminded me of a conversation I had had with an English businessman in London. I had used the word 'truth' and he had stopped me in the middle of my sentence. 'Truth!' he had exclaimed. 'What an interesting word. I don't think I've heard that word since I was a boy.' He then added the sad words, 'After all, no-one today believes in truth, do they?'

As Christians, however, we follow a Saviour who claims to be not only the way and the life, but also the truth (John 14:6) and he has given us the Spirit of truth (John 14:17; 15:26; 16:13). Truth forms a central plank in the content of the biblical revelation, and the welfare of society at every level is dependent on the practice of truth.

After we had left the sheikh's house, Aziz laughingly told me that Sheikh Omar had come to him for help concerning marital issues. 'He already has three wives, but has now fallen in love with a very pretty young girl whom he now wants to take as his fourth wife.' Aziz went on to explain that in the sheikh's Egyptian culture, it is not permissible to take another wife without the permission of the previous wife. 'His third wife is quite a strong-minded American lady,' he told me. 'She refuses point blank to authorize a fourth wife who will supersede her in the family pecking order. American women don't bend to their husbands' wills as easily as our Pakistani girls.'

'How does the American wife feel about her Muslim marriage?' I asked, knowing that Aziz was close to the whole family and the sheikh's wives might well confide in Aziz' wife.

'In traditional Muslim marriage,' Aziz explained, 'the men find their companionship with other men, while the wives look to other women for their friendship and support. But in American and European marriage, the husband and wife expect to be companions and friends to each other as well as fulfilling their marriage responsibilities.'

I realized that it must be hard not only for the American wife of the sheikh, but also for other Western women married to Muslim men. Their expectations in marriage would be so different. It would be easy for the Muslim husband to feel his wife was too demanding and self-willed, while the Western wife might feel lonely and dissatisfied with a relationship which included very little true companionship or communication.

On the other hand, some Western women are reacting against the sexist looks and comments which they sometimes receive at work and on public transport. The thought of being totally covered in shapeless clothes and being protected by their husband may be attractive, although it goes right against the concept of freedom which is so important to most of us. The fact that quite a few Western women convert to Islam challenges our whole value system. In the context of a very insecure society and of a thrusting, self-seeking culture the Islamic emphasis on obedient submission can act as a magnet. The very word 'Islam' means submission and applies not only to their attitude towards God, but relates also to women's approach to their menfolk, whether a girl to her father or older brother, or a wife to her husband.

As Aziz and I were talking, his older boy came home from school and quietly entered the room without disturbing our conversation. After a while, Aziz turned to his son and asked him how the day had been at school. 'No trouble today, I hope,' he added.

Turning to me, he explained that his eleven-year-old son was facing real opposition and even some violence at school. Most of the other boys were Muslims and did not like having a committed Christian in their class. Perhaps too they were a little jealous because he was bright academically, shone at all sports and had been chosen by the staff to be head boy of the school. He was finding particularly that the short walk home from school was an ordeal. Several times he had been attacked by groups of boys, while more often he was just jostled and verbally abused.

'It's really all right,' the boy said, smiling at me. 'I'm a Christian and expect some trouble with the crowd of Somalis and other Pakistani kids.' Having myself been badly bullied as a Jew at school by anti-Semitic boys, I admired his quiet confidence and his willingness to suffer for his faith. He had evidently not hidden his light under a bowl (Matthew 5:15), but was allowing it to shine and give light to others.

While staying with Aziz, it was a privilege to speak in various churches about witness among Muslims. Before one such evening meeting, the minister shared with me that they felt God was calling them as a church to witness more definitely to the many Pakistani Muslims living around their church.

'We've started by distributing a copy of a Gospel to each home,' he informed me.

'That sounds excellent,' I replied. 'Which Gospel have you been using?'

He told me that they had been using Mark's Gospel, the usual starting point for British non-Christians.

'Mark is most suitable for British people,' I commented. 'It's straightforward and simple, and gives the basics of the life, death and resurrection of Jesus. But it's unsuitable for widespread pioneer evangelism. The very first verse declares that it is "The beginning of the gospel about Jesus Christ, the Son of God". Muslims strongly reject the idea of Jesus as God's Son, so most of them won't read beyond the first verse of chapter 1.'

'So which Gospel should we use among Muslims?' the minister asked.

I commented first that the Gospel of Matthew is very Jewish and assumes a knowledge of the Old Testament, so that is also unsuitable for Muslims, or non-Christian English people who also know little of the Old Testament. 'On the other hand,' I added, 'Matthew can be good because it starts with the genealogy of Jesus. In most Muslim cultures, people's true identity will be ascertained by their family background.' When first meeting each other, they will normally recount where their family comes from originally, who their parents and grandparents are. This contrasts with Westerners, who introduce themselves by stating what they do professionally and perhaps where they live now.

John's Gospel, I went on, is well suited for Muslims who

belong to a mystical Sufi group. But it assumes that its readers will already know the basics of the life of Jesus. Muslims believe in Jesus as a great prophet, but they know very little about the details of his life or teaching. 'The Muslim Jesus,' I said, 'is like a skeleton without flesh. Through the reading of a Gospel we hope they may be able to add flesh to the skeleton. It's hard to relate to a mere skeleton, so it's important that their knowledge of Jesus becomes more human.'

Perhaps Luke represents the most appropriate Gospel for a Muslim to start with. At the time of Muhammad, Christians in his area of Arabia did not normally use the New Testament Gospels. They preferred the Diatessaron, which takes parts of all four Gospels and combines them to form one composite whole. The Diatessaron is particularly based on Luke's Gospel, and Muhammad himself gained much of his knowledge of Jesus through Christians who were using the Diatessaron. As a result, Muslims may feel more at home with Luke's Gospel than with the other Gospels. It is closer to Muslims' beliefs about Jesus, although inevitably there will still be much which clashes with an Islamic understanding of him. Luke begins with the birth stories of Jesus, including various accounts of angelic appearances. Muslims believe firmly in angels as God's messengers of revelation, so that appeals to them. They also believe in the virgin birth of Jesus, so the birth stories may give them a feeling of confidence to read further. However, all the Gospels focus on the cross and resurrection of Jesus. Muslims deny Jesus' death and therefore also his resurrection, although they believe in his ascension into heaven.

Sadly, however, it may remain difficult for any Muslim to read even Luke's Gospel, for all the Gospels stress the death of Jesus on the cross as the climax of his life and work. All the Gospels also imply the divine nature of Jesus as God incarnate, which is totally unacceptable to Muslims unless the Holy Spirit is working sovereignly in them.

In talking with the minister, it was clear that he and his church were still at the very beginning of their new adventure. Previously their evangelism had been among their fellow British, with little attempt to reach out to their Muslim neighbours. Their witness with the white English people near their church had prepared them for the greater challenge of evangelizing Muslims, for their church members were largely those from professional, middle-class backgrounds, and university students. The people living around them, however, were mostly less educated and more working class, so they were already having to practise a form of cross-cultural witness. It is not easy for an edu-cated middle-class church to reach out effectively even to British people who are from a different social context. Such churches need help and would benefit from further training in cross-cultural mission.

In the modern globalized world, most churches will have people of various ethnic backgrounds in their vicinity. Even in our conservative village in rural Hertfordshire there are Bangladeshis, Chinese, an Ethiopian, Afro-Caribbeans, a Philippino, a Cuban, an Iraqi and a Turk as well as myself as a Jew. Such international contexts present all our churches with major questions. Should all such recent arrivals in Britain just adapt and fit into the traditional British back-ground with British forms of communication and worship, British approaches to Scripture and theology, and British styles of leadership?

Of course, within the loving fellowship of the Christian church, it is incumbent on us all to make everyone else feel comfortably at home, so when ethnic minorities become Christians, they will do their utmost to fit into the local church despite cultural differences. But in evangelism it is the task of the Christians to sit where their non-Christian friends sit. It is up to us to adjust our ways to make the gospel relevant for the people we are attempting to reach for Christ.

'Is it really wrong for us to put our Bibles on the floor in our church?' someone asked me recently. 'I know we have lots of Muslims living around the church, but should we adjust our ways to fit them even though it's quite rare for anyone who is still a Muslim to come into our meetings?'

'When you're in a meeting where you have several Muslims and the whole meeting is seeking to relate to them,' I replied, 'then it may be good to show respect for the Bible in their way. But usually we can continue to behave as normal British Christians always do. If we try to adjust to all the different religions here, we shall quickly realize how impossible that is – Muslims, Sikhs, Hindus, Buddhists and followers of Judaism. You cannot possibly please them all, so why single out Muslims? Do we concentrate on Muslims just because we feel they cause more trouble than others? If so, that's wrong.'

It is of course most helpful that many former mission workers from overseas are returning home to work among ethnic minorities here. They have a good deal of experience of the cultures they have worked with overseas. They will have learned the language of the people among whom they served. And people from those countries now living in the West will be excited to chat with them because they can talk together about the places in Africa, Latin America or Asia from which they came. Such former missionaries will almost certainly have a natural rapport with immigrants from their part of the world.

Some former missionaries relate particularly to overseas

students. At present they appear to be just ordinary students, but in the future they may well hold significant positions in their home countries. It is important that they should go back home with a positive impression of the Western country where they have studied. And if they can be reached for Jesus Christ and brought to know him, they will prove to be the best possible missionaries in their home countries.

Other former mission workers come back to their home church and join with them in their mission work and outreach. Despite the fact that Muslims in Europe differ in many ways from those elsewhere,[1] with their experience from abroad ex-missionaries can be a real help to local believers in learning how to evangelize among people of a different culture and religion.

With the huge number and diversity of ethnic minority people in the UK, it is particularly important that we mobilize and train the local churches and Christians for cross-cultural evangelism. They will be living, working and studying with people from all over the world. So they are the natural instruments for God to use in evangelistic witness in our multi-ethnic, multireligious world.

Reflect
How can we explain the importance of truth in our contemporary context?

Is monogamy essential for Christians or just God's biblical ideal? How would you advise a polygamous family who wanted to become Christians?

7. DR ABDUL: LIFE IN A MULTIFAITH WORLD

The noise and bustle of the London traffic was muffled by the double-glazed windows and the heavy damask curtains. My host had already warned me that he had invited a Muslim fellow doctor for afternoon tea. 'He's an excellent doctor and we get on very well,' he explained, 'but I long for him to become a Christian. I pray so much for him, but somehow we seem to get nowhere when I venture to talk about Jesus.' He went on, 'He seems to have everything. He doesn't appear to need anything and is quite content the way he is as a rather nominal Muslim. He's doing well professionally; he has a lovely family with a beautiful wife and two delightful children. In fact, I always really enjoy visiting him. There's such a lovely atmosphere in their home and they're so hospitable.'

On his arrival, Dr Abdul settled easily and comfortably into a large armchair. He made himself quickly at home and with his perfect Queen's English engaged me in thoughtful conversation about all manner of social and political issues of the day. His intelligent eyes held steady behind his discreet glasses as he looked without embarrassment directly into my eyes. His up-to-date silk tie went perfectly with his neat pink shirt and the stiff cuffs at his wrists displayed a smart pair of cufflinks. His black trousers were beautifully creased and his shoes gave everyone a clear sense of the good-quality leather from which they were made. He had obviously given his shoes a good polish before coming out, for the toes gleamed in the reflected light, showing off the elegant sophistication of the good doctor.

As I observed his manner and chatted with him, I thought to myself, His patients will have no doubts in trusting Dr Abdul when he gives them their medical assessment and treatment. We were comfortably seated in a pleasantly furnished sitting room with a warm fire burning and a goodly supply of cakes and biscuits to accompany the very English cup of tea. Dr Abdul was evidently very much at ease in this well-off, middle-class environment.

Our conversation took place in the month of Ramadan, when many of us as Christians were praying for our Muslim friends and for the whole Muslim world at this special time of fasting. But Dr Abdul showed no hesitation in enjoying our afternoon tea together. He quietly explained that he did not normally observe the fasting month or pray at the set times, although he still considered himself a Muslim.

'Many of my patients are Christians, but they don't practise their religion,' he informed us, 'and I'm a bit like them. I'm a Muslim, but I don't observe the religious forms of my faith.' He gave us a confident smile, feeling that he had happily put us at our ease in inviting him to share food with us during Ramadan.

'You don't practise your faith, so what does it actually mean to be a Muslim?' our host asked with a slight air of bewilderment.

'Although I feel entirely at home among English people in this country,' he shared with us after a little thought, 'I very much belong to my own Pakistani community. They are mostly Muslim and I therefore relate to the Muslim umma, the people of Islam. Generally speaking, their friends are my friends and their enemies are my enemies.'

As our conversation ranged around many different topics, it was evident that Dr Abdul strongly supported the Palestinian cause against the State of Israel. Indeed, he became almost heated as he denounced what he felt to be the gross injustices of Israel and bemoaned the oppressed plight of the Palestinian refugees. I observed that whether religiously practising or more nominal in their faith, all Muslims seem united in vehement opposition to the State of Israel. Although the unity of the umma is based on the *Tawhid*, the oneness of Allah, some people wonder whether that unity would survive without their common enmity against Israel. Without this political situation, the world of Islam might fragment in violent fighting amongst its own people.

My mind moved on to the subject of Christian unity as the people of God, brothers and sisters with the same Father. Does our unity depend on having a common enemy? Opposition to particular moral sins can bind together Christians of different theological persuasions. Fear of the fundamentalistic intolerance of politically correct pluralists in the church, Government, media and our wider society can also force us to stand shoulder to shoulder with Christians with whom we might otherwise have considerable disagreement.

Nevertheless, the New Testament teaches us that we have more important foundational reasons for unity. It is essentially our faith in Jesus Christ as our one Lord and Saviour which holds us together in love. As believers, we all have the one Holy Spirit dwelling within us. We share the same sure hope of the vindication of the Lord's glory, holiness and love in the ultimate future when Jesus will come again in his majesty and splendour. So we find our unity as Christians in our common faith, love and hope. This positive foundation allows for a deeper fellowship than just the negative fact of a common enemy.

Both Christians and Muslims need to check themselves.

On what foundation does their unity as the people of God stand?

It was interesting getting to know Dr Abdul further. He not only shared the political emotions and attitudes of his fellow Muslims, but, as he told me, he could also quickly adjust his behaviour to fit his more traditional Muslim family. When he visited his elderly parents or his wider family, he fitted easily into their context, but on returning to the more English context of his immediate family and his work, he unhesitatingly snapped back into a middle-class British form of behaviour. Dr Abdul was typical of many second-generation immigrants in any part of the world. He lived happily in two cultures, adjusting naturally and easily from one to the other.

Sometimes, however, his two worlds jarred with each other. In his university and medical studies he had learned to relate with open-minded tolerance towards all beliefs or points of view. Together with many Westerners, he had come to feel that we have developed a 'supermarket mentality', where each customer has the right to choose the goods they personally prefer. No-one stands up in the supermarket to preach that their preferred type of cheese or biscuit is the only good or healthy one. Likewise this multicultural philosophy declares that all cultures have equal validity, so it is wrong to seek to persuade one's neighbour to change and follow some other world view. With this he had also taken on board the criticism about Christian foreign missionaries – that they destroyed the former way of living of the peoples among whom they worked.

So pluralism undergirded much of his academic thinking. But his upbringing as a Muslim had taught him something quite different. Although he no longer prayed or fasted, only very rarely attending a mosque, he still maintained much of the fundamental thinking from his childhood. He therefore asserted without hesitation, 'Islam is of course the final revelation from God, the one true faith. It comes after Judaism and Christianity, so supersedes them.' He seemed quite unaware that his words might offend us in any way and calmly continued, 'Religions like Hinduism, Buddhism or Sikhism with their belief in various gods and idols feel a bit primitive, don't they?'

I found myself wondering how such assumptions could coexist alongside his sophisticated pluralism. The two seemed so obviously mutually irreconcilable!

'Do you believe in the truth of the shahada [the traditional creed of Islam]?' I asked as we delicately munched crustless sandwiches. 'Do you feel that belief in Allah as the one and only God can be reconciled with an easy tolerance towards your Hindu associates? And how do you handle the fact that other religions reject Muhammad as God's greatest prophet and messenger?'

Enjoying a handsome slice of home-made chocolate cake, Dr Abdul gave me a smile and pointed out that some Hindus accept Muhammad too as an avatar (an incarnation of a god, in this case Vishnu). He seemed oblivious of his previous dismissive rejection of Hinduism as primitive. 'But of course,' he added, 'Muhammad is more than just another avatar.' He then turned his well-educated attention to Buddhism, pointing out that 'Buddhists too are sometimes happy to accept that Muhammad came to possess the Buddha spirit, or even that he was one of the many reincarnations of the Buddha'.

I pointed out that Buddhists would be fitting their belief about Muhammad into their philosophical system and asked, 'Can Muslims actually accept that Muhammad is just another incarnation of the Buddha?'

Our charming, sensitive hostess sensed that a theological

argument might spoil the pleasant atmosphere of our tea together. She quickly offered us all another cup of tea and Dr Abdul gratefully gave her his cup. He didn't seem to worry too much that other religions might not agree with his Muslim faith. Tolerance still prevailed.

Of course, it will always remain true that every true Muslim must strongly oppose the Jewish and Christian rejection of Muhammad as a prophet. The Muslim view of Muhammad will always clash with even the most tolerant or accepting Jewish or Christian understanding of the person of Muhammad.

It was not easy to ask Dr Abdul about the evident discrepancy between his Westernized pluralism and his more traditional upbringing as a Muslim. It felt almost intolerant to push him into facing these two mutually contradictory systems of belief. 'I'm sure the two can be reconciled somehow,' he smiled when I did eventually suggest that Islam and pluralism seemed to be so different. Another cup of tea seemed the ideal solution to the problem.

My conversation with Dr Abdul touched also on the great topic of the Qur'an. How does it relate to the Bible and to Jesus Christ as God's revelation?

Dr Abdul remembered his childhood teaching on Islam and replied as if by rote: 'We Muslims believe in four major books which God has revealed through his prophets. The Taurat reveals God's Law and came through the prophet Musa [Moses], so I suppose it is almost equivalent to your first books of the Old Testament which claimed to come through Moses. This represented God's Word in those early days, but through the rebellion of God's people this first revelation became inadequate.' He paused for breath and another sip of his tea. He clearly felt proud of the learning he had gained so many years before. 'So in due time

God caused another book, the Zabur [Psalms], to come down to humanity through the prophet Da'ud [David],' he continued. 'Everything in the Taurat plus much more was then to be found in the Zabur, so the former Taurat became redundant. Again, unbelief made it necessary for God to replace the Zabur with another greater book, the Injil [Gospel], which came to humanity through the prophet Isa [Jesus].'

Dr Abdul hesitated for a moment, seeming to wonder whether he was stepping on to dangerous ground with us, but nevertheless ploughed on. 'The Injil contained all that had previously been in the Zabur together with a yet greater revelation, so the Zabur was no longer needed as God's Word.' He began to look somewhat embarrassed as he repeated the teaching his mullah had given him in his youth. I felt he was beginning to question how this traditional teaching, which he had always unthinkingly accepted, could be squared with his wider friendship with Christian friends. Bravely but perhaps a little unwisely he continued. 'The Christians had sinned in developing what we Muslims believe to be the heretical doctrine of the Trinity with Jesus as God's Son, so God replaced the Injil with the most glorious and final revelation of the Qur'an.'

With a renewed confidence he declared, 'Sadly, the three earlier books have been corrupted and their original texts have been lost. But it's not really a problem, because happily all the wisdom and truths of God which were previously found in the other books are now even more wonderfully displayed in the Qur'an, which abrogates all previous revelations. The Qur'an is so miraculously perfect in truth, wisdom and beauty. No other revelation from God is in any way needed or even useful.' He delivered his final conclusion with definite satisfaction, settled back comfortably in his armchair and concentrated on the piece of cake which had been forgotten during his little lecture.

Surprisingly, I thought to myself, throughout the history of the church some Christians have entertained a theological understanding which is almost parallel to this Muslim approach. They believe that God has replaced the Old Testament with the New Testament, so the earlier covenants of God are no longer relevant or valid for us as Christians.

Such theology is highly dangerous, I told myself, for God's promises are irrevocable (Romans 11:29) and his grace continues to be offered to us despite our sin and rebellion against him.

If Israel's sin had caused God to withdraw his covenantal promises to them, then the church would have little assurance of God's continuing grace to Christians. My mind wandered back to the anti-Semitism which has often prevailed in the history of the church.

I reminded myself of what I believed: The record of the church, as indeed of each one of us personally, is also not without sin and rebellion! No, the new covenant in Jesus Christ is the goal and climax of the old covenant with Israel. There is a definite continuity between the old and the new covenants. The New Testament in no way cancels out the Old Testament. The church is the continuation of the congregation of Israel, but now with Gentiles added into it also (Romans 11:11–21). God's covenant now relates not only to Israel, but also to Gentile believers in Jesus who are grafted on to the Jewish olive tree. So in the Christian faith there can be no question of one revelation or covenant replacing and disqualifying any previous word or promise from God.

Dr Abdul could still remember what he had learned about the Qur'an and the earlier books of God when he was a youngster. But he had never compared his traditional Muslim teaching with his present tolerant acceptance of other religions and their beliefs. In conversation it soon became clear to him that as Christians we held firmly not only to the New Testament Gospels, but also to the Old Testament Law, Psalms and Prophets.

So I gently told Dr Abdul, 'Christian belief in the whole Bible can never be reconciled to the Muslim view that the earlier books have been replaced by the Qur'an.'

He seemed genuinely shocked that our two faiths could be in any way opposed to each other. 'Are you really suggesting that both the Muslim and Christian beliefs cannot both be equally true?' He shook his head in disbelief at such an outrageous suggestion.

Another contradiction soon reared its head as I chatted with Dr Abdul. I dared to ask him in what way God revealed his Word.

Dr Abdul put his childhood teaching into words: 'I was always taught that God himself wrote the Qur'an in heaven before the creation of the world. Muhammad was illiterate, so surely he could never have written such a glorious book as the Qur'an. He was just the channel through whom God sent down his revelation. But the Qur'an was eternal and uncreated.'

My mind went back to John's introduction to his Gospel. With Dr Abdul's background in a good British public school, I assumed he knew the beginning of John's Gospel, so I voiced my thoughts. 'Christians too believe that the Word, Jesus, was with God even in the beginning. So both Christians and Muslims hold that the Word preceded all creation and was indeed uncreated and eternal. Then in the fullness of time God sent the Word into the world.'

Dr Abdul nodded in agreement, obviously reassured that

indeed our two faiths could happily coexist. It was not easy to go against his tolerant pluralist approach, but I felt I had to add, 'The difference is that in Islam the Word became a book, the Qur'an. In the Christian faith God's Word became a human being, Jesus Christ. In Islam the eternal Qur'an never was God although it was eternally with God and uncreated, whereas in the Bible "the Word was God"' (John 1:1).

I tried to explain to Dr Abdul that in our Christian belief, God's revelation has both divine and human elements. Jesus himself is entirely God and yet at the same time he becomes incarnate as a fully human person. Likewise the Bible is not only 'God-breathed', inspired of God (2 Timothy 3:16), but it is also written by fallible human beings like Isaiah and Jeremiah, Matthew and Mark. Because the Bible is written by human authors, its message bears the imprint of their characters and personalities, their historical contexts and beliefs – and yet by the overruling inspiration of the Holy Spirit the revealed Word remains entirely perfect.

Dr Abdul listened with rapt interest, desiring to under-stand what we as Christians believe. With his tolerant attitude, he so wanted to understand.

A sad look came into his eyes as he regretfully apologized. 'I'm afraid I find it so hard to understand how God's revela-tion can be both human and divine. And as a Muslim I find the Christian idea impossible that Jesus could be God on earth and not just a great prophet.'

Then a new thought came to his rescue. 'But of course, lots of Christians don't accept the Bible as being in any way from God. And my religious education teachers at school didn't believe that Jesus was born of a virgin or was somehow God.'

Dr Abdul very much wanted to be able as a Muslim to

agree with people of other religious faiths. Mutual tolerance was for him the bottom line. His polite pluralism did not allow him to disagree openly.

As we parted, he was happy to receive a copy of the Bible and he promised to study it carefully. He assured me that his mind was open to everything, still feeling that somehow his Muslim understanding could stand together with Christian beliefs. If he ever becomes a committed believer in Jesus Christ, he will face the same battle the other way. Both true Muslims and Christians believe in the absolute uniqueness of their faith. How then should we affirm an assured faith in Jesus as the way, the truth and the life while at the same time demonstrating a genuine rejection of all intolerance and arrogance? It is a challenge.

Reflect

How should we as Christians view other faiths? Are they demonic and untrue, or another way to God – or something else?

8. WALKING IN THE SANDALS OF THE JUDGES: MEETING THE QADIS

The telephone continued to ring insistently. It was a considerable time before my host strolled into the sitting room to answer it. But I was not in any way concerned about the telephone, for as a mere visitor to this Middle Eastern country without any public speaking programme, few people would know that I was in the country and no-one would know with which friends I would be staying. It seemed that my visit was low key and anonymous.

As the phone droned in the background, I had therefore pressed on with the book I was quietly reading. Life seemed very relaxed staying with these friendly Christian workers in their comfortable flat. And I always flourish in a warm climate with the stimulus of a different lifestyle, foreign foods and the challenge of thinking through the gospel of Jesus and the life of the church in another cultural context.

'It's for you, Martin.' My host's words jolted me out of my reading and thoughts. Still surprised at being called to the phone, I duly acknowledged that it was me speaking and then asked, 'Excuse me, but to whom am I speaking?'

'This is the chief qadi speaking,' came the shocking reply, which sent a frisson of nervous apprehension coursing through my veins. The qadi is the Muslim judge who is responsible for all pastoral issues and legal affairs in a Muslim society. The chief qadi usually plays a significant role in teaching Islam in the media, for he will be an authority not only on matters of Muslim law, but also on the teachings of the Qur'an and the Hadith.

During the time of Muhammad, his followers would sometimes come to him with their problems and uncertainties. If he did not yet have an assurance of God's revealed will on the subject, he would often ask people to go away for a time while he asked Allah to reveal his will on the matter. This is the background for some of the verses of the Qur'an as we have it today. But then Muhammad died and people wondered how they could discover the will of God in situations for which the Qur'an had no clear answer. It was agreed to collect all reliable memories concerning the life of the prophet as God's model for his people.

For Sunni Muslims these traditions carry the authoritative weight of God's revealed will, for Muhammad is believed to have been the ideal messenger of Allah. Everything known about his life reveals to his people the perfect will of Allah for his people.

And now in our day the qadi teaches the law of Allah and applies it both in the personal lives of his followers and also in Muslim society as a whole. He is therefore a very important person in Muslim society.

So I wondered how the chief qadi of this Middle Eastern country knew of my presence in his territory. And what did he want of me? Why was he phoning me? Was I somehow in serious legal trouble? My nerves tingled as I awaited his further words.

My shock and apprehension turned rapidly into icy horror as the qadi informed me that he had read my book, *Islam and Christian Witness*. My mind raced to some of the threatening comments sent to me by Muslims in response to this book. One letter had demanded that the book be withdrawn and pulped. If I did not remove it from public circulation, the letter continued, I would suffer all the agonies of hell. It then listed in great detail the number of times my eyes would be raked by demons per day, per year and per million years. It went on to affirm how many tongues of flame would lick me how many times and other such hellish tortures. These threats were balanced by more mathematical tours de force as the author determined how many beautiful brown-eyed virgins I would be able to enjoy if I did in fact withdraw my book. Likewise he calculated how many golden goblets of wine I might enjoy each day, each year and in a million years.

Various warnings have also been posted on the net with reference to this book. So I shivered with some anxiety when the qadi coolly informed me that he had read this book. Trouble surely threatened.

But then he said that he would like to come to where I was staying, in order to meet me. If he had wanted to interview me officially in his position as the qadi, he would have summoned me to a meeting in his office. I knew therefore that all was well. I could relax.

At the appointed time he stood at the door. Dressed from head to foot in white traditional Muslim attire, the qadi's rotund body was topped by a jovial round face which split easily into a warm smile. He appeared like a Muslim version of Friar Tuck. I could imagine how Muslim couples coming to him for marriage advice or other pastoral needs would have felt quickly at ease.

Seated comfortably in an old-fashioned armchair in my host's sitting room, he immediately relaxed. I noted with interest that he even sat with crossed legs, a sure sign to me that I too could feel happily at home with him. And yet I continued to be very aware that this easy-going man in front of me also represented the highest Muslim authorities in the land. I reminded myself therefore that I should not be careless in what I said or did in his presence.

'I read your book with interest,' he started after we had exchanged pleasantries for a while. 'Of course you describe Islam from a Christian perspective,' he continued, 'and I found myself disagreeing with what you said about Christianity. I cannot accept your Christian views on the nature of God and the so-called Trinity. As a Christian you also stress the death of the prophet Jesus on a cross. That goes absolutely against our Muslim beliefs.'

His comments sounded so basic. Surely he had not wanted to meet me just to point out that as a Muslim leader he did not accept my book's descriptions of the fundamental beliefs of the Christian faith. What was the real purpose of his visit? Why had he wanted to meet me?

After a little pause for reflection he then said quietly, 'I felt, however, that in your book you walk in our sandals. That is why I wanted to meet you.'

I did not tell him that my ethnic and cultural background has much in common with that of the Arabs and therefore with Muslims generally. I just told him that I had had the privilege of living for many years in Muslim societies in South-east Asia and various local Muslims had graciously accepted me as a friend. Some of them had shared quite intimately with me and allowed me to gain insights into the soul of Islam, not just its outward forms. 'I have learned much from my Muslim friends,' I concluded, 'and I hope that some of them through friendship with me will have gained more understanding of the glories of the Christian revelation.' I did not want through my politeness to give the impression that we as Christians have much to learn from Islam, but that Muslims have nothing to gain from us Christians. But I also did not want to show the qadi that my calling was to work as a missionary, witnessing to Muslims with the definite aim that they might come to faith in the

Lord Jesus Christ as their Saviour and as God incarnate on earth.

Ever since my talk with this qadi I have often used his beautifully descriptive expression 'walking in our sandals'. In teaching about Christian mission we need to encourage people to learn the other people's world view, religion and culture so that they do indeed walk in their sandals, sitting where they sit, thinking with their thoughts, dreaming their dreams and empathizing with their ambitions.

What a privilege it was to share with this man in more detail why I as a Christian hold fast to the central truths of the Christian faith. In our further conversation I was able to explain why we believe that the death of Jesus is central. I hope he caught a glimpse of the glory of the sacrificial death of Jesus for the sin of the world and for our sin personally as individuals. I was able to tell him a little about the life-changing reality of the resurrection of Jesus which gives us as believers the joy of a totally new life in Christ. And then I went on to the amazing gift of the Holy Spirit who in John's Gospel is known as the Spirit of truth; he demonstrates in the Acts of the Apostles his power through his disciples and throughout the Bible he works within us as the Holy Spirit to bring his divine holiness into our lives.

This is not the only qadi with whom I have enjoyed a close rapport. Another time, pointing me to a tall man with a slight stoop, a conference secretary very quietly informed me that this man was the leading qadi of his country – a different country from that of the qadi above. I observed him with interest, although no opportunity came at first for any more personal interaction. Each day of the conference he wore casual Western-style clothing of unobtrusive colours, such as brown and grey. His hair was receding, leaving a dignified bald area above his forehead. He was obviously keeping himself slightly apart from the other participants in the conference and he gave a definite impression of being somehow different from the rest of us. He had come alone to the conference, so there was no sign of whether he had a wife and children or not. But he did not seem to mind being a bit on his own, although he behaved with gracious politeness towards the very international group of Christians at the conference.

In the times of open prayer he prayed with earnest faith and with insightful biblical and theological content. The depth of his faith became apparent in his prayers and one could see that here was a man of profound biblical understanding.

The conference secretary confided to me, 'The qadi is a baptized Christian believer, but he keeps it very secret from other Muslims. Actually, he is still working as the chief qadi of his nation and still represents Islam on TV and radio, giving the Qur'anic teaching. But in his teaching he constantly uses the Injil, the New Testament, and holds up the prophet Isa [Jesus] as our ideal model for life.' She then went on to tell me that many Muslims in his country suspected that he was a secret Christian, but he always managed somehow to avoid their probing questions. With other Christians, however, he was quite open about his faith in Jesus.

Aged about fifty he held himself with confident yet humble maturity. Finally, after one of my talks, he came up to me quietly, introduced himself and suggested that we go to his room to talk and pray together.

In his room he told me about his family. 'My wife became a Christian before I did and I owe much to her gentle testimony. I was struck by the change in her life when she became a Christian and I saw a new light in her eyes as she began to develop a spirit of gracious serving.'

What a lovely couple they must be, I thought to myself. His mature graciousness coupled with her humility and loving ministry of service would surely combine to make them an outstanding couple who would demonstrate the beauty of Jesus Christ in their Muslim country and society. And I imagined a man of his calibre representing Islam in the media as a committed, baptized Christian, promoting the supremacy of Jesus.

What a predicament this couple faced. If he openly declared his faith in Jesus Christ, not only would he lose his position as the qadi and the wonderful opportunity he had to speak of the Injil and Jesus through the media, but also he would certainly have been murdered, for in Muslim eyes the penalty for such so-called apostasy is death.

On the other hand, biblical teaching makes it clear that our heart must be expressed in our lives and in our words. So Paul declares that 'if you confess with your mouth. "Jesus is Lord," and believe in your heart that God raised him from the dead, you will be saved' (Romans 10:9). Can it be right therefore for anyone to remain a secret believer? Inevitably their words and perhaps even their outward religious practices will sometimes fail to confess their faith that Jesus is the risen Lord. But to choose to face certain martyrdom is no easy decision.

'Every day I face the pain of how our situation is affecting our two daughters,' he confided, his anguish reflected in his eyes. 'They have also become definite believers in Jesus, so they don't want to marry Muslim men. The Bible is so clear in its teaching that Christians should not be yoked together with unbelievers' (2 Corinthians 6:14). I could see the pain etched on his face as he continued, 'You will understand that they are officially still Muslims, so by Islamic law they cannot legally marry a non-Muslim man. So they have both determined to remain single and never to have the joy of marriage and a family of their own – and I shall never have grandchildren.' I gathered later that his two daughters were both in their early thirties, which is late for a woman to get married in Middle Eastern culture. And in their country it would be considered a shame that neither of the women married and had children. While rejoicing that this whole family had found eternal life in Jesus Christ, at the same time I felt a real sadness at their predicament. In strongly Muslim societies, Christian converts from Islam face enormous suffering whether they remain secret believers or whether they come out openly as followers of Jesus as the incarnate Son of God.

On another occasion the qadi graciously pointed out to me that I had referred in a talk to the reality of Islamic jihad as the basis for some Muslims' violence. I had also used the common English translation of it as 'holy war' and mentioned suicide bombers, murder of Christian converts and aggressive fighting in places like northern Nigeria, Indonesia and Afghanistan. Quietly the qadi reminded me that there are two forms of jihad in Islamic theology.

He wanted to stress that even the more aggressive form of jihad should only be in defence of Islam when the oneness of Allah and the call of Muhammad as God's prophet are attacked. He wanted to maintain this emphasis firmly although he was well aware that Islamists follow the teachings of the Muslim Brotherhood in considering even moderate Muslims as the enemies of true Islam. They feel justified therefore not only in showing violence towards non-Muslims, but also against all Muslims whom they feel are compromising the full faith of Islam. The qadi knew too that these Islamists consider everything and everybody in the West to be fundamentally opposed to Islam, so

such occurrences as 9/11 are to them merely in defence of
Islam against what they see as the imperialist aggression of
America and Europe.

But he particularly emphasized the other form of jihad,
which developed later in the history of Islam. This describes
the experience of struggle (the previously mentioned literal
meaning of jihad) between good and evil within us all. His
concept of jihad paralleled Paul's teaching that 'the sinful
nature desires what is contrary to the Spirit, and the Spirit
what is contrary to the sinful nature. They are in conflict
with each other, so that you do not do what you want'
(Galatians 5:17, see also Romans 7:7ff). This emphasis on
the inner jihad of the heart holds a central role particularly
among Sufi Muslims.

Sadly, I never met this qadi friend again, and it was
obviously unwise for me to keep in contact. I have often
wondered what happened to him. Did his Christian faith
bring him into further suffering or even martyrdom?

Reflect

Is it biblically allowable to remain a secret believer?

What might it mean for you to 'walk in their sandals' when
it comes to Muslims?

9. MUHAMMAD, ALI AND THE WHIRLING DERVISHES: EXPLORING SUFISM

'They were amazingly conservative,' one of my Bible college students commented to me after working for a while in a very traditional evangelical Christian bookshop in the Midlands of England. 'They wouldn't even stock the books of C. S. Lewis because those weren't sufficiently evangelical to pass their test. And they considered more liberal commentaries or books entirely beyond the pale,' she added.

But then to my surprise she told me about some of the Christian posters they stocked with biblical verses or other helpful quotes on them. Some had devotional words from Hindu or Buddhist scriptures, but also one or two cited deeply spiritual concepts from such poets as the Sufi Rumi from Turkey. The owners of the bookshop did not know other religions sufficiently well to be able to discern where such quotes came from or who the authors were, so they felt happy to stock posters with these words on them. To them they seemed attractively devotional. The conservative evangelical managers warmed to the Sufi emphasis on an intimate relationship of love with God, failing to discern that Rumi and other Sufi poets are still entirely Muslim in their faith.

Standard Sunni and Shia Islam stresses the absolute greatness of Allah, the one who is distant from us and who is totally other than his creation. As a result the transcendent greatness of God stands above any idea of the immanent nearness of a loving Father God. Most Muslims may therefore experience the reality of God's active sovereignty in the world and in support of his Muslim people, but may not enjoy a closely personal and intimate relationship with God on an individual basis.

In reaction to this emphasis on the distant greatness of Allah, the Sufis underline the immanent closeness of Allah. It is the Sufis who have produced beautiful Islamic devotional poetry, lovely miniatures in painting and various forms of art which glory in the splendour of nature.

Having no knowledge of God as the Trinity, however, both the ordinary Sunni and Shia Muslims and the mystical Sufis find it hard to keep together the fact of God's indescribable, unattainable greatness and his loving presence with us which allows us as mere weak human beings to know him through an intimate personal relationship.

My first visit to Kabul, the capital of Afghanistan, took place in 1980 when the Russian Communists had just invaded and taken over the Government. This resulted in ferocious fighting with horrendous atrocities on both sides. In consequence it became a highly dangerous place for white foreigners, who could easily be mistaken for Russians. The police would also apprehend any Afghan who was seen talking with a foreigner who was not Russian.

Not fully appreciating the dangers, a German friend, Albrecht, took me down to the old market to see the sights. As we began to pass through the brightly coloured stalls it was soon obvious that the local people were reacting with undisguised hatred. Were we going to have a knife in our backs? 'We are not Russian, we are English,' my friend called out repeatedly in the local language. The scowls gave way immediately to smiles of welcome.

Having been in Kabul for some years and speaking the language fluently, Albrecht was well known locally and much respected. Many of the stallholders greeted us from a distance and we waved back with friendly gestures. 'They wouldn't want us to stop and actually meet them, for it's much too dangerous,' Albrecht advised me. 'So we'll just wave our greetings and pass on quickly.'

But then an old man, Muhammad, insisted on coming down from his little cloth stall to greet us more closely. He duly kissed us on both cheeks with the traditional five kisses.

'Our friend leads a Sufi group which I attend,' Albrecht explained. I later discovered that he not only went fairly regularly to that group, but would chant portions of the Bible and Christian prayers or hymns in their worship times. In this way he not only developed a close relationship with his Sufi friends, but also was able to have a definite witness among them. So he was known and respected as a Christian Sufi.

'Is your friend a true believer in the living God?' the Sufi leader, Muhammad, asked.

Albrecht affirmed to him that I was indeed a believer.

'Please share with me how you came to faith in the living God,' Muhammad requested. In those dangerous times of suffering he needed to know whether I could be trusted.

I began to tell him how at the age of fifteen God had worked a miracle on my behalf in direct answer to a specific prayer and as a result I had come to faith in the Lord. 'Yes,' he exclaimed exuberantly, 'we are brothers! I too turned from mere book religion and became a believer in the living God when I was fifteen.' With a sense of joyful anticipation he urged me to tell him more.

'I became very religious at that time,' I went on, 'but it wasn't a great success. Then when I was twenty years old, a fellow student at university showed me that it wasn't what I did for God that counted, but what Jesus had done for me.'

'Wonderful!' Muhammad declared and then astounded me with the declaration, 'When you see Jesus, you see God;

when you know Jesus, you know God; Jesus is the way to God. We are brothers indeed.'

I soon discovered, however, that as a Muslim he still rejected the divinity of Jesus, and also his cross and resurrection. He knew nothing of the Holy Spirit of God, so the whole idea of the Trinity remained totally alien to him. But as a Sufi he could admire and love Jesus as the perfect mirror image of God, believing that through his relationship with Jesus as the ideal, wonderful prophet from Allah, he could come into a personal knowledge of God. He was obviously a deeply spiritual person, a man of prayer and warm devotion.

'As fellow believers in the God who is alive, I insist that you come up into my cloth stall and that we drink tea together.' Muhammad beamed with delight at the prospect of fellowship with us. He then sent a boy to buy a kettle of tea and some sweetmeats. Solemnly we sat together on the red carpet in his little cloth stall.

'Normally I would invite you to come to my house to eat and drink together, and to share fellowship in prayer,' he explained by way of apology. 'In these times, however, that would be suicide. But at least with fellow believers one must share tea together. For this I may only be tortured.'

I could not help admiring him. His faith in God meant so much to him. He radiated a confident and joyful love for God. But I was also very much aware that I would never have risked torture in order to share fellowship with him. I was not even sure that as a Christian I would consider him a brother or fellow believer.

Later, when we came away, I began to ask myself serious questions. Could this Muslim be saved through his clearly inadequate understanding of Jesus? How much does one need to know about Jesus in order to receive eternal life? The cross and resurrection of Jesus are the very heart of the gospel, so could this man be born again without these central truths?

I had to think through this whole experience. I came to see that ultimately it was not my responsibility to judge whether this man, with his particular degree of faith in Jesus, was saved or not. God is the judge, not us. But God calls us to preach the fullness of the gospel to all people, whether they may already be born again or not. Muhammad was missing the central glories of the Christian faith; he had no assurance of salvation and no knowledge of God's forgiveness of all his sin. The wonder of the Holy Spirit remained an unknown mystery to him. He still lacked so much in his faith.

As I looked back on my encounter with Muhammad, I thanked the Lord for the opportunity of meeting a man with such courageous faith. I noticed too that his love for Jesus made him more open than most other Muslims to hear the message of the incarnation of Jesus as God's Son and the atoning work of Jesus on the cross.

What a privilege to be allowed to share something of the fullness of the gospel with such a man! Yet at the same time I felt humbled by his radiant spiritual life and love for Jesus, which banished even the fear of torture.

This experience reminded me of a Sufi friend back in Britain. Ali was getting old by the time I met him in the north of England. Once a week his group met in his home for an evening's worship. The men sat on cushions around the wall on one side of the room, while the women faced them from the other side. At each meeting, they would have a protracted time for different members to chant a prayer or a section from the Qur'an and then the music would begin. It started soft and slow, but quickly gathered speed and volume, with rhythmic clapping to encourage people to stand up and dance. Sometimes the dancers would end in a trance and fall senseless to the floor with the belief that the spirit of Allah was coming specially to them.

'When we all first came across to England,' Ali reminisced one time, 'we Pakistanis were poor, coming mostly from simple village backgrounds.' His eyes misted over as his mind went back to the 1960s and somehow it felt as if he was no longer living in his present world and home. 'We could not afford to build a mosque or hire the services of a Muslim teacher or leader. So we just met in our homes unofficially and informally. Having no proper imam or mullah, we soon found ourselves forming Sufi groups which we could run ourselves.'

Bringing him back into the present, I commented, 'Now, of course, the Muslim community has more money and power, so it can bring teachers over from Pakistan and other Muslim countries. You have large and beautiful mosques in most of the cities with large Muslim populations. And you have many small mosques or prayer houses for the smaller groups of Muslims.'

He wagged his head sadly and admitted, 'Yes, things are not the same now. Muslims from Bangladesh, Afghanistan and so many other countries have come. It was so nice when we were just Pakistanis, all speaking Urdu and all with the same background.' After some thought he then added, 'And now the younger generation has introduced radical politics into our community and they have lost the spirituality and humility of our Sufi form of Islam.' [1]

Tears welled up in Ali's eyes as I shared with him how my two daughters have followed in their parents' foot-steps as followers of the living God and Jesus Christ, but have adapted our patterns of faith to fit their more modern context. 'And now we begin to see our grandchildren com-mitting themselves to follow God as Christians. We pray that our faith and love for God will progress from generation to generation into the future.'

Ali was deeply grateful when I offered to read a passage from the Bible and to pray with and for him. He was hungry for spiritual warmth, but could not yet see how the life of the Spirit could fit into the modern world. Life was changing all around him, but he was still existing in the simple faith he had known in the past. It also grieved him to see the disorientation of so many Muslim young people in Britain today. He could not understand the gang culture and crime which had become so common among young Muslims in his area.

My wife and I felt this same tension between the Sufi spiritual life and the realities of the modern world when we were visiting Khartoum in Sudan. 'Would you like to go outside town to see the whirling dervishes?' our hosts asked us. 'They hold their worship regularly out in the desert.'

We had of course read of the whirling dervishes, but had never encountered them in the flesh. I had talked of them in lectures, but had never myself attended a dervish session. So we eagerly looked forward to the experience.

Across the desert came the troop of Sufi dervishes, reciting sections of the Qur'an to the accompanying playing of their band. At the accepted place they stopped and got themselves ready. Their band played softly and slowly, while a growing crowd of us gathered in a large circle to watch the worship.

Dressed in traditional Turkish-style trousers and top, one man sauntered into the middle of the open space in the centre. Slowly he began to revolve round and round, following the music. Then other men joined him and formed lines like spokes from the hub. As the music increased in volume, speed and emotional intensity, the man in the centre twirled round faster and faster, with his arms outstretched. Each of the other men also spun round and round as individuals, while at the same time each line was rotating like the hands of a clock. The crowd joined in with rhythmic clapping, encouraging the worshippers in their dancing. An atmosphere of spiritual power came upon the crowd and the dancing worshippers. One by one, people began to fall into a trance and lie on the ground.

Elizabeth and I sensed that this was no mere tourist performance, despite the crowd of people watching. The reality and power of spiritual forces was evident. As we prayed for these people in the glorious name of Jesus Christ, we longed to be able to impart to them the knowledge of the true Spirit of God. We wondered what effect the Sufi worship of the whirling dervishes would have on their lives at home and at work in the city. With the Holy Spirit, God gives us power unto holiness within the world, not just out in the desert.

Jesus declared that God the Father had sent him into the hurly-burly of everyday life in this world (John 17:18) and he affirmed, 'I am still in the world' (John 17:13), although he was about to leave it (John 17:11) and return to the Father. So in John 17, Jesus also sends his disciples into the practicalities of this world (John 17:18) to live the Holy Spirit's distinctive life of holiness, and by the Spirit to share with the world God's gift of eternal life which comes through knowing 'the only true God, and Jesus Christ, whom you have sent' (John 17:3). The life of the Spirit is very down to earth.

Reflect

In what ways should our lives of holiness be distinct from the world around us?

How could you ensure a good balance in your thinking and attitude between being aware of the purity and greatness of God, and of his graciously loving relationship with us?

10. TARIQ AND HUSSEIN: AFGHAN STORIES

'We have lost so much of our history,' Tariq commented to me with a sigh. Although he had been in England now for a couple of years, he still dressed in the Afghan manner and was particularly attached to his traditional brown headgear. His English had improved, but lacked a wider vocabulary and grammatical accuracy. His accent betrayed his particular Afghan background. Being already in his forties, it was not easy to adjust to a totally different way of life as a refugee in England. Whenever possible he wandered along to the homes of other Afghans who lived within easy reach of his own home in the English Midlands. Here he could talk his own language, drink tea in an Afghan manner and eat foods to which he was accustomed. With these friends he could relax and feel at home.

When he discovered that I had been to Afghanistan a couple of times and had observed a little of their history and culture, Tariq gave me a warm welcome. Although we were in England, he had no hesitation in greeting me with the traditional kisses. It never occurred to him that this might in any way be misunderstood in Britain, where homosexual practice is so much to the fore in people's minds.

As Tariq bemoaned the loss of so much of Afghanistan's history, he began to think back to the terrible days of internecine fighting after the Russians had been evicted from the country with terrible losses. 'The different groups of mujahidin [Islamic guerrilla fighters] fought each other without any concern for the welfare of our nation or people,' he commented. 'They destroyed almost every worthwhile building in Kabul and the centre of the city was flattened.'

I added something from my own memory. 'Yes, all those old war memorials have vanished off the face of the earth.' How well I remembered the strange feeling I had had when standing before those monuments which gloried in the utter defeat of the British invaders and the slaughter of our armies when Britain and Russia were struggling for supremacy in that part of the world during previous centuries.

'It could have been helpful if the American and British leaders had been able to see those old war memorials before they ventured into Afghanistan to fight the Taliban,' I observed, and he agreed. 'They might have learned a lesson before they committed their troops to fight against locally based militias. But somehow we never learn from history.'

In my mind I pictured the wild mountainous terrain of the Kabul Gorge and the Khyber Pass, where guerrilla warfare will always prevail over standard military strategies. At one stage in the Kabul Gorge the road juts out from the sheer rock face and is supported by man-made beams. As one looks down, coil after coil of the road can be seen snaking its way to the bottom. Later, as one heads towards Jalalabad and Pakistan, the road is lined with the burned-out wrecks of Russian military vehicles and tanks which were ambushed and destroyed by the mujahidin during the war with the former Soviet Union. Did the Americans and British understand what they were going into when they sent their troops to such a country with its long history of intertribal warfare of Sunni Muslim against Shia Muslim, as well as against one invading army after another?

When we began to discuss the present troubles back in his home country, Tariq became quite agitated. He declared with considerable bitterness that the Americans and British should get out of his country and go home. How dare they invade his country, poking their noses in where they were not wanted! Their presence, he felt, was just provoking more warfare and more destruction. His people were even poorer than they had been before and the whole of society had been disrupted. His English stumbled to express his feelings, but it was not difficult to discern what he wanted to say.

As is true of so many Afghans, Tariq's vehement faith in Islam undergirded everything in his life. Although he was generously hospitable and agreeable in his personal friendship with me, it never entered his mind even to consider the possibility of leaving Islam and being converted to the Christian faith. He would listen politely and even with some interest when I shared about my faith in Jesus Christ and what that means for me. But it was clear that his assured faith in Islam, Muhammad and the Qur'an never in any way wavered. To him it was obvious that Islam is the one true faith, infinitely superior to all other religions. He therefore found it strangely obtuse on my part that I had remained a Christian and not accepted Islam. 'Why don't you become a Muslim and follow the true path of God?' he would ask me from time to time with a mystified shake of his head.

To Tariq, Christianity was a militaristic and aggressive faith which constantly aimed to destroy his country and people. He associated the very word 'Christian' with the anti-Muslim crusades, the long centuries of imperialist aggression, the so-called 'Christian' nations' attacks on Iraq and his own country. He hated the Americans particularly for their support of the State of Israel, which he thought of as the great enemy of Islam. Although he knew little of the arguments for and against the existence of the State of Israel, he assumed that all Muslims should be united in the passionate desire for its destruction.

Because Islam was the foundation for everything in Tariq's life and thoughts, he presumed that Christianity must motivate everything that Americans and Europeans do. Their policies and actions in his country and in the Middle East must stem from their Christian faith, so he confidently believed that Christians are therefore working for the destruction of Islam. The immorality of our media, he assumed, was an expression of Christian values and beliefs, seeking to undermine the moral standards which Allah had revealed in the Qur'an and Hadith.

'Your patterns of education just instil constant doubt in the minds of young people,' he accused me. 'Your teachers don't have the authority to teach truth to their children. In this way you attack our clear and certain revelation which shows us the truth in all things. We don't want our children to think things through for themselves, as if there was no certain revealed truth. Our religion tells us everything we need to know and it is the teacher's job to instruct on those things with definite authority.'

So he would affirm that Western politicians, media and education have the one great aim of bringing Islam and Muslims to their knees. To me, it seemed that a real siege mentality ruled in his attitudes. Christianity was thus fatally linked to Tariq's reactions to America and Europe. And as he hated the West, so he reacted in the same way to Christianity.

On the other hand, many Afghan refugees in Western countries have suffered from the violence and hatred of their fellow Muslims back in Afghanistan. As a result many have become disillusioned with Islam and, in the freedom of the West, they have become open to the message of love and forgiveness in Jesus Christ.

'Are you a Muslim?' screamed an Afghan man above the whistle of bullets all around them. He had come across a Western Christian worker outside on a road in Kabul.

Bombs, rockets, shells and bullets were devastating the city. Fear and ferocity were etched on his face as he gripped this unknown foreigner by the lapels and shook him.

The expatriate Christian thought his end had come. Surely he was going to be killed. He trembled as he declared that he was a Christian, not a Muslim.

'Promise me that you will never become a Muslim!' the man shouted and shook him again. It was an easy promise to make!

We can only imagine how that Muslim had suffered from the fighting of the various Islamic factions against each other. Terror and violence was wrecking the whole country and the lives of multitudes of families and individuals. No wonder some began to question the validity of Islam and wonder whether God might not have provided some better way.

Such Muslims are naturally more open to the gospel when they come into the relative peace and freedom of the West.

In those same times another expatriate Christian worker was driving through the streets in the midst of the fighting when he was stopped by an Afghan man in the middle of the road. Was he going to be hijacked or killed? the Christian wondered. But then the man shouted to him, 'Get me out of this country! I don't mind where you take me – as long as it is not a Muslim nation.'

Evidently this Afghan too had seen the intolerance of fundamentalist Islam. We should not be surprised that most Afghan refugees strive to get to America or Western Europe, if possible. They do not make their way to Saudi Arabia or the other Muslim Middle Eastern nations, despite their wealth and the material possibilities open to Afghans as fellow Muslims.

At that time of ferocious fighting, the central mosque in Kabul had a problem. On one Friday at midday prayers, almost no men turned up for the salat. The leaders sent armed men into the city centre and around the old market to round up the men and force them to come to the mosque for prayer. Hundreds filed into the mosque under the threat of Kalashnikovs.

'You can force us into the mosque,' some of the men declared as they stood at the back of the room, 'but you can't force us to pray.' Around two hundred men stood, obstinately not praying, despite the danger of what might happen to them afterwards.

The Qur'an may affirm that 'there is no compulsion in religion', but in such circumstances theory and practice do not coincide. Again we may wonder what those men will feel about Islam. Will they have open ears when they hear the gospel in a country where they are free from the pressures of society and of their own Muslim families?

So it is that Afghan churches and groups are springing up in various countries in Europe as well as in America. Even outside Afghanistan and in the apparent safety of a democratic country, they still feel danger from their Muslim neighbours. They fear that Muslim governments will discover their existence and murder them. They are well aware of the common Muslim belief that Islamic law (shariah) demands death for all who commit apostasy from Islam. Some Muslim lawyers query this interpretation and deny that the death penalty should be applied to apostates, but in practice, people who convert from Islam to another faith in a Muslim country will often be killed. So even in countries like Germany or Britain, fear lingers in the hearts and minds of Afghan Muslim converts, as indeed is also true of Muslim converts from many other ethnic backgrounds.

'I've had enough of Islam,' Hussein declared to me with considerable force. Proud of his athleticism and muscle-building prowess, his lively eyes flashed with a never-resting energy. His English had improved rapidly as he had given himself to a good study of the language. He was determined to fit into British life and society, and not to remain obviously ethnic and risk being a background misfit. He had abandoned his traditional Afghan garb and stood tall in jeans and casual shirt. Culturally too he wanted to adapt to British ways. He watched how English people reacted to things, what they talked about, how they related to each other and generally how they lived. He wanted to be as English as possible. Life back in Afghanistan was the past. Life had moved on for Hussein.

'Tell me about your years in Afghanistan,' I nevertheless urged him one day.

He began to tell me of the terrible hatred and fighting there had been between the different factions after the horrendous war against the Russians with the shocking cruelty of their atheistic communist regime. No Afghan Muslim could tolerate their atheism even before they let loose the horrors of their campaign of terror. And now with that experience of the Russian invasion, atheism was absolutely anathema to all Afghans.

'And after the Russians it became even worse. When our Muslim groups began to fight each other, every building in Kabul was damaged. The main places like the royal palace and the national museum were entirely destroyed. The centre of the city was flattened, so that it was impossible to recognize where one was in that area.'

It was obvious that he could not easily wipe the past out of his memory despite his desire to forget Afghanistan and become entirely British.

After the period of internecine fighting the Taliban had come in. At first, many people had thought that they were going to bring in a new era of peace after the horrors of civil war. True religion with an emphasis on prayer, devotion to Allah, godly morals and harmony would surely now reign supreme. But the sinfulness of human nature had prevailed. Cruelty and despotic pride had ruled in the name of Islam and the shariah.

'If that's true Islam, you can keep it!' Hussein almost wept as his eyes showed painful memories flooding in. 'The Taliban told us so confidently and proudly that their ways are the only true form of Islam; all other Muslims are just compromising. They forcefully taught us that we all needed to follow the law of Islam in the minutest detail.' He went on to remember with bitterness the sufferings of Afghan women at that time, how the men had to grow their beards or be beaten publicly on the street, how traditional kite-flying and games like football were forbidden on pain of death because they were not in the Qur'an.

'But they flaunted their rockets and Kalashnikovs,' Hussein smiled unhappily, 'and they are also not mentioned in the Qur'an.'

Hussein told me how he had heard of a man in the city of Jalalabad whose house had been searched by the Taliban for no apparent reason. They had discovered a copy of the Christian Bible in his house. Although the man had quite forgotten that he had ever been given the Bible and he was in no way a Christian, the Taliban leaders had taken him out and hung him from the nearest lamp post.

'When I heard about this, I began to wonder whether Christianity and the Bible might teach a better way than the Taliban and Islam,' Hussein whispered. 'But in those days under the Taliban I could not even mention such a thought to anyone, so it just remained as a vague idea in the back of my mind. But I never entirely forgot it.'

Then Hussein had taken the opportunity of escaping from Afghanistan and slipped across the very porous border into Pakistan. From here he had gradually made his way across to Europe and to England, the land of his dreams. Here an English friend had offered him a copy of the Bible, that book which had raised many questions in his mind but which he had never actually seen or read.

'My friend told me to begin with Luke's Gospel and showed me where to find it. I was amazed to read all sorts of details about the birth of Jesus which I had never heard as a Muslim. As Muslims we also believe in the virgin birth of Jesus, but we know very little about it. And the stories around his birth are full of angels. As a Muslim I knew that angels are the ones who bring God's revelation, so I began to see Jesus as God's messenger and Word. Then Luke's Gospel teaches such wonderful things about the life and relationships of Jesus as well as what he did.' Hussein went on to tell me about his first impressions as he read about the last week of Jesus' life on earth, his death on the cross, his glorious resurrection and ascension.

Then the book of Acts followed. The stories of the first Christians thrilled and inspired him: the wonder of the first Pentecost and the coming of the Holy Spirit to the disciples, the message of the sermons both to the apostles' fellow Jews and also in Acts 14 and 17 to foreign Gentiles – indeed, the spread of the good news of Jesus far and wide both to Jews and Gentiles. He was so gripped and fascinated by it all. Then one day he suddenly thought to himself, I am believing all that! I am like those first followers of Jesus! I too am excited by all that Jesus is and does. I must be a Christian.

His English friend was overjoyed when Hussein told

him that he thought he was now a believing Christian. The two of them then began to read the New Testament together and their fellowship blossomed. Soon Hussein was introduced to other Afghan believers in Jesus Christ and he began to attend a local Afghan church. This was also part of a larger English church, so Hussein could relate to English Christians as well as other Afghan believers.

Let us never forget that the Holy Spirit of Christ is working wonderfully among Muslims in our country today as well as overseas. And surely God wants us to share in what he is doing, for we are called to be his fellow workers. In his Journal, John Wesley remarks that it is our task as Christians to bend our backs to second and assist the work of the Holy Spirit.

Reflect

How far do you think ethnic minorities should adapt culturally to the country where they are now living?

Do our hymns and songs seem to support the common Muslim perception of Christianity as a religion of militaristic aggression?

11. CONNECTING WITH CHRISTIANS: MAKING THE MOST OF TOURISM

'Why do you have an Arabic book by your bedside?' the woman who had been cleaning our room each morning asked with an air of uncertainty. She obviously found it beyond her imagination that a Western tourist should have a book in Arabic. 'Can you read it?' she asked.

Staying in this tourist hotel before we went on to give Bible readings in a conference for Christian workers in a North African country, we had purposely brought with us an Arabic Bible which we left on our bedside table each day. When the cleaning lady had done our room each morning, we noticed that the Bible had shifted its position somewhat and we wondered whether she was reading a bit of it whenever she could be alone in our room, before or after cleaning it and making our bed.

'Would you like to have the book?' I replied. 'You're welcome to it. We're leaving today and can easily get another copy when we return to England.' She was delighted at our offer and accepted. We had already affixed the address of a Christian organization in England inside the Bible, so that she would have an outside contact if she had further questions.

When we left the hotel later that morning, we placed the Bible on the dressing table together with our tip. Meanwhile we had also taken the opportunity of giving a copy of a Gospel in Arabic to the man working in the little boutique where we bought postcards, and also to the man who served us our meals in the dining room of the hotel.

Christian tourists abound in some of the countries of

North Africa and the Middle East. We believe that God has a special purpose for us when we go to Muslim countries either as business people or as tourists. Surely his desire is not just that we do good business and rake in the money, nor that we merely revel in the luxury of warm swimming and lazing in the beauty of the sun-soaked beaches. Our times of relaxation and holiday are also an important part of God's gracious provision for our welfare. God is pleased that we should enjoy our holiday and relax from our normally busy schedules, but as Christians we are never on holiday from our faith. God's call to mission remains valid even when we are lounging on the beach or by the side of the swimming pool. We believe that everything we are and do is all part of God's call to us. We are called to serve him at all times and to be his witnesses wherever we go.

'It would be wonderful if Christian tourists could make a point of discreetly distributing Christian literature when they come to our country on holiday,' declared a Christian leader to us as we shared fellowship with him in a seaside tourist town. 'In our Muslim-dominated country, we Christians are watched very carefully by the police. They know everything we do and it is highly dangerous for us to give a New Testament or other Christian literature to a Muslim.' He then told us with seriousness, 'I have been interrogated several times by the police because I have witnessed to a Muslim or given them some Christian book or tract. But our country desperately desires as many Western tourists as possible to come here. Our national economy depends very much on tourism. So the police are very careful not to cause offence with tourists. As a result, you are free to do things which are almost impossible for us as local believers.'

Then he smiled broadly. 'Christian tourists may nevertheless be wise to wait until the final day of their holiday before they give out their Arabic Christian literature. Otherwise they might be expelled from the country unexpectedly and might share the fellowship of some suffering with us! But if they are just about to leave the country anyway, the police will just allow them to go and will be glad to see the back of them. They may not even know that the police have been watching them carefully in the hours since they gave someone a Gospel. Please tell Christians in your country what I have said,' he begged us.

We were challenged by his heartfelt words and could well understand their significance. Small groups of Christians face considerable opposition and even persecution in most Muslim countries. They feel their weakness as a tiny minority surrounded by a sea of Muslims. And their every movement is noted by the police. The slightest false move can bring them into serious trouble.

I was reminded of his words one day after preaching in a large Anglican church in England. Richard, a parishioner, came to talk with me afterwards. While most people in the church wore casual clothes, he was smartly dressed in a tailor-made suit and matching silk tie while his face gleamed with aftershave. His hair was immaculately styled and he walked with the confident bearing of a professional man who was highly respected in his work. He stood out as a leader among men.

'I travel frequently to the Middle East for my work,' Richard informed me purposefully and it was obvious that he wanted to ask something serious. 'I meet regularly with the top people of the country where I go and I am often invited to their palaces for dinners and feasts. It is also my privilege to be invited to their desert picnics, which are sumptuous occasions.' He smiled at the memory of these luxurious gatherings, which bore no similarity to the informal picnics common in England. 'In my work I also have to discuss matters with the highest leaders of Islam in the country, the top sheikhs and qadis.' His work involved him in the most prestigious Muslim institutions whose names are known throughout the Muslim and even the non-Muslim world. I blinked in amazement that a committed Christian could be employed in such central Muslim areas with such vitally influential contacts and relationships.

'How could I share my Christian faith in such a context?' he asked and his clear-cut love for Christ came across without hesitation. With no embarrassment he then confessed, 'Until you spoke this weekend, I had assumed that I could not mix work and witness. In my professional assignments in the Arabic-speaking world I have served my company, but I have hidden my faith for fear of it damaging my company's position in that part of the world.'

'Of course you do indeed have a responsibility to your company not to bring it into disrepute by unwise witness, although you must long to grasp with both hands the opportunity to share Jesus as Lord and Saviour with such top people in the world of Islam,' I commented. 'You need a combination of wisdom and boldness which is not easy to hold together. But you may be the only Christian who will ever have the opportunity to share the good news of Jesus and his salvation with them.'

I reminded him that the apostle Paul was particularly concerned for 'boldness'.[1] In summary I added, 'The Greek word *parrhesia* signifies a clear and definite assurance of truth which then motivates one to confident and brave witness. In your position you will need a wise boldness based on a deep, quiet assurance of truth – quite a combination!

'There is something you could do in the way of witness when you are invited to dinners in the homes of these top people in society. It is customary in such circumstances that the guests should bring a gift to the host.' He nodded in agreement, for this was evidently his experience too. 'You could perhaps sometimes offer your host a New Testament gift wrapped in smart paper and ribbon. As you present it humbly and politely to your host, you could ask him whether he would do you the honour of accepting a copy of your holy book.' With a chuckle I then added, 'Don't do this too often, so that you begin to be known as one who is distributing New Testaments to all and sundry. Carefully and prayerfully choose just one person you feel would be open enough to receive your gift and would appreciate reading the Christian Scripture.'

Christian visitors to such countries should generally avoid all contact with local believers or mission workers from overseas, if they want to give Christian literature to people with whom they have contact. Otherwise it is very possible that these Christians working locally may have trouble with the police after the tourist or business person has left the country. The foreign Christian will leave the country, while those left behind may be blamed for what the foreigner has done. It is helpful if the local workers can honestly declare that they have had nothing to do with these visiting Christians and cannot in any way be held responsible for what they may do.

Wealthy Muslim leaders often want the opportunity to read the Bible, although it may be forbidden in their country. For example, Muslim men flock across the causeway into Bahrain at weekends to buy what cannot easily be obtained or what is banned in Saudi Arabia. The rumour is that they return home with a bottle of whisky under one arm and a Bible under the other! Forbidden fruits always have a special appeal. So it is often the case that our offer of a New Testament or a Gospel may be gratefully received.

These are readily available through the Bible Society in whatever language is appropriate. Of course, we can also recommend that such people get hold of a Bible on the net or just read it on the computer screen.

Evangelistic witness and distribution of Christian literature are not the only ministries available to visiting Christians from overseas, as we discovered during a visit to North Africa.

'Isn't it wonderful?' exclaimed our new friend. She and her husband were the only foreigners living in this North African resort where we were enjoying a short holiday. 'For the first time in all history the Holy Spirit is specially present in our town here.' My wife and I looked at her with considerable uncertainty and wondered why she was getting so excited. She had not seemed to us to be someone who was prone to exaggerated emotional outbursts.

'This is the first time ever that Christians have gathered in this town to worship the Lord,' she continued. 'The Lord has promised that he is specially present among his people when two or three are gathered together in his name.' With a lovely mixture of seriousness and joy she reminded us again that there had never before been any Christian witness in that particular area and that there were still no converts from the local Muslim population. Of course, our friends had worshipped the Lord regularly by themselves, but this was the first time any form of wider worship had been held there.

Coming from the freedom of England, for us it was nothing out of the usual to worship together with our friends that Sunday morning in our hotel bedroom. But now we joined them in the excitement of making history. And we have more recently been encouraged to hear of a good group of local Christian believers which has come into being in that town. Our little gathering with the four of us was the harbinger of greater things to come. The Holy Spirit of Christ was indeed present there in a special way that Sunday!

Before going on our holiday we had contacted a mission agency to ask whether they had members working in that town. We had then made discreet contact with them and arranged for them to come round to our hotel to meet us. Being the only Christians in that whole area, it was encouraging for them to have fellowship with visiting Christians. And they much enjoyed the luxuries of our hotel. Lounging under umbrellas by the side of the swimming pool was not their usual routine as pioneer mission workers!

We could not only give them fellowship and a small taste of luxury relaxation. They also added considerably to our holiday, for they took us out with them to visit people in a nearby town. For us the bus trips were interesting and we gained much insight into local life through our visits with them to homes. Lunch in a simple café in a small town added to the interest. The tagine of stewed lamb and vegetables, served under a conical clay cover, tasted delicious. We then wandered through the narrow streets, admiring the high mud wall surrounding the town.

Such an excursion makes a wonderful change from swimming and sitting on the beach or by the hotel pool. As tourists it is very easy never to learn anything about the local life and religion, but with this couple we could gain many new insights which added colour to our holiday and would give fuel for prayer in the future.

We realized anew that Christian tourists can have a ministry of encouragement in the places they go to. And the tourists too will gain blessing from their contact with the overseas Christian workers there.

In some situations, tourists and business people may also

have the opportunity of encouraging local Christian believers. We must never forget, however, that we need to be particularly careful in Muslim countries, for police observation and severe persecution often threaten. If we are seen visiting anyone, trouble can quickly fall on their heads. But we felt free to invite this couple to our hotel because we were just on holiday and carefully avoided other Christian activities which the police might have noticed.

Our new friends were foreigners like ourselves and it would appear natural that we should get together in the context of a swim in the hotel and an outing to local villages. But other local believers might be hauled before the police and roughly treated for associating with them. The religious authorities and even their own families might attack the local believers, using the accusation that they are collaborating with foreigners in the underhand introduction of an alien religion. They might even be accused of working together with the CIA and other foreign spies, for Muslim leaders often believe that overseas Christian workers are in the pay of the CIA. We may dismiss this as patently ridiculous, but it is amazing how frequently this accusation recurs in country after country.

Nevertheless, there remain situations where it is wonderfully helpful and encouraging for overseas Christian tourists or business people to meet with local Christians to give them fellowship. In this way we can give them the assurance that they are not forgotten by the wider Christian church worldwide. How exciting for such lonely and isolated Christians to discover that they really are a vital part of the international body of Christ! Brothers and sisters in other countries are indeed praying for them in their life and witness.

It was in a small town in north China that we met with the leader of the local Christian group. He could hardly take it in that believers from overseas were actually meeting with him in his rather remote city. His gnarled fingers and weather-beaten wrinkled face betrayed the long years of suffering and opposition he had endured for his faith as a Christian. He had survived the horrendous persecution and torture he had endured under the Red Guards (the mass movement of students during the Cultural Revolution in the late 1960s). And when we met, the authorities were still making life difficult for him and for the little church he was trying to lead. He had kept body and soul together through the years by working as an untrained dentist, pulling teeth on request. We rejoiced to spend time in prayer and fellowship with this brother in Christ, but were glad that we did not have to submit our teeth to his mercies!

When we assured him that there were Christians in our country who had prayed for the church in his city right through the years since the Communists took power in China, tears welled up in his eyes. That one visit from us had broken through the thick wall of isolation he had suffered for many years. He had always felt his inadequacy and lack of biblical knowledge as he led his little group of believers, but now he knew that he was supported by other people's prayers. Surrounded by hostile authorities and the overwhelming multitudes of unbelievers, he had always allowed his difficulties to destroy his sense of the Lord's peace and rejoicing. But now he could face these difficulties in a new way, for our presence with him spoke of the fact that he was a vital part of God's sure purposes for his church and people worldwide. He was not alone.

Our new friend insisted that we must celebrate our fellowship together with lunch in his simple home. He sent someone to buy take-away food and we sat down together to a sumptuous Chinese meal. As also in the Bible, in

Chinese and Muslim cultures, eating together has deep significance and we rejoiced not only in the deliciously tasty Chinese food, but specially in what this meal meant to our new friend as well as to us. The lines of care on his face began to relax.

Occasionally as visitors we may even have the opportunity of giving a little much-needed teaching in the fellowship of local believers. One time a message came through to my hotel bedroom: 'The leading elder of the local unregistered Baptist church will come to your hotel room this afternoon.' Central Asia was at that stage still under the domination of the Russian communist system. In this Baptist church both the ex-Muslim believers and the Russian Christians were meeting secretly. But they had good contact with a former Bible College student of ours who was working in that city. He had informed the leading elder of the church that we were visiting the city and advised him to invite me to give some teaching in the church.

In their Central Asian situation, they were beginning to recover from the atheistic propaganda of the past and Islam was gaining ground again. Many people felt that their identity lay in their Muslim roots. So our former student felt it could be useful for the Christians to have some biblical teaching which related to Islam. Such unregistered churches wanted to be sure that they only invited people of clear Christian faith, who would not teach anything contrary to the doctrine of the church.

The elder duly arrived in my room at the specified hour. 'Shall we go for a short walk in the park opposite?' I suggested, knowing that most hotel bedrooms were bugged by the secret police.

'Certainly not,' he replied with no hesitation. 'They have already put me in prison three times and if they want to do so again, they are welcome.' He glowered in the direction of the ceiling corner where he thought the bug might be placed.

He then proceeded unceremoniously to put me through my theological paces. 'What do you believe concerning the Trinity? What is your view on the atoning work of Christ? Is the Bible the inspired Word of God? What is your experience of the work of the Holy Spirit?' He fired one question after another, weighing my answer to each one. Finally he declared curtly, 'I see that we are brothers. You will come to our meeting at 10.30 on Sunday morning and preach. We shall then ask you our questions and you will give us teaching.' On this he stood up and left the room without any polite farewells or pleasantries.

I wondered what sort of man he was. Why was he so abrupt? Why did he lack Christian graciousness and any normal politeness? Later, when I shared my bewilderment with our former student, he explained that this man's father had been a church leader and had been sent together with all the other church leaders to a Gulag in Siberia for years when this man was just a small boy. Only the women remained and none of them had a job to support them all and their families. The elder's mother had had to leave the house early each morning to try to find little jobs which would pay for basic food for her six small children. Each morning she would put what food she had on the kitchen table alongside an open Bible with the words, 'You will not be alone. God will be with you.' Then she would leave home for the day and lock the door for safety, only returning late in the evening.

Our elder friend had therefore never known adult relationships throughout his childhood and youth. His one outing from the home had been to church each Sunday where he would sit through the adult service and teaching.

There was no children's work as such. No wonder he had none of the little skills of interpersonal relationships which most people learn as children with their parents and other adults.

However, as a visitor in a foreign country, it is often we ourselves who are the learners. The enormous challenge of their sacrificial discipleship of the Lord humbles those of us who come from the relative ease and comfort of being a Christian in Western Europe or America. Is the love of Jesus Christ truly more important to us than comfort, security and position – even than life itself?

My faith was bolstered as I walked to their church that morning. Along the side of the road lay a tangle of uncared-for long grass with a considerable accumulation of rubble, rubbish and general mess. To my surprise, at one stage, I found a quantity of rusty metal. On examination it quickly became clear that this used to be a communist slogan which had stood atop one of the buildings or on a billboard by the side of the road. With casual curiosity I deciphered the now nearly illegible writing: 'The words and deeds of Lenin live for ever!' the Russian text declared with assurance. But now they were just a rusty tangle of old metal in the rough grass along with all the other rubble and discarded rubbish.

At the church that Sunday it was a real privilege to preach and then to answer one question after another on the teaching of the Bible. The little handful of Muslim converts had their particular questions, while the Russians came at the Bible from their angle. For them all it was a rare opportunity to get more teaching from outside their own circles and from someone with more biblical and theological training. Although they read their Bibles avidly and were steeped in biblical truth, they lacked knowledge of the history of biblical times and were also not accustomed to consecutive biblical exposition which could look at the overall teaching of a whole Bible book and relate it to an Islamic context. They were hungry for teaching and excitedly received all I could give them.

At the church and on meeting the unregistered Baptist Christians there, it was immediately evident that they were financially poor and mostly uneducated. However, they had withstood the power of the state and the media through more than seventy years of atheistic propaganda, discrimination and persecution. As Christians they had been forbidden to have regular jobs; the whole educational system had taught militant atheism, and society around them had attacked them for their faith in God. But despite everything that had been hurled against them, they had won the battle. The legacy of Marx and Lenin had crumbled into a heap of rusty metal, but the faith of Jesus Christ had stood firm and had triumphed.

We pray that this same faith in Jesus Christ may also persevere and be victorious all over the Muslim world. Often the small groups of Muslim-background believers in Christ seem fearfully fragile in the face of the surrounding sea of Muslims with all their confident declarations of the superiority of Islam. But we believe that the glory of the Lord shines in weak and earthen vessels; his power is manifest in and through weak and ordinary disciples. We follow a Saviour who changed the world for ever through the suffering and humiliation of his death on a cross, not through worldly power.

Reflect
What could you do to help with Christian mission when visiting a Muslim country as a tourist or for business?
Should we try to visit local Christian believers or churches when we visit a Muslim country? What are your reasons?

CONCLUSION

Cracks in the fortress: times have changed

'Christian mission among Muslims is like a small boy with his toy bow and arrow. Facing the boy looms a huge old English castle with thick stone walls and a surrounding moat. The boy shoots a little wooden arrow against the mighty walls of the fortress; it hits the wall, makes no impact and falls uselessly into the moat.'

That was the picture with which I often began when leading seminars on Islam in various churches and conferences. Happily that picture is now no longer true. In those days, however, I would continue by adding, 'In mission among Muslims we need workers with patient endurance, love and a strong sense of hope in the Lord's ultimate victory.'

Having worked in Indonesia for some years when my wife and I served as missionaries in East Asia, I knew that there were one or two major exceptions to the rule which my illustration of the boy with his bow and arrow described.

In our time in Indonesia, God was working in amazing ways. The church with its 5 million members was growing at that time by about 10% a year with large numbers of Muslims turning in faith to Jesus Christ. Although the particular churches we served with were largely working among people of tribal religion, many Muslims were also being converted.

'The people of my village were so open when I began to tell them about my new-found faith in Jesus,' said Madany, a tall, muscular lad in our youth group in North Sumatra.

He belonged to a people which was at that time still entirely Muslim. But during his college holidays he had returned home and shared his faith with evident fruitfulness. Soon a new church emerged with about a hundred converted Muslims.

'I feel very inadequate,' Madany shared with me when he returned. 'All these new Christians are looking to me to lead them, and I'm just a beginner. They need to be formed into a proper church. And I don't know how to do it.'

Whereas Madany's people had been entirely Muslim and the church was new, in other parts of Indonesia the church is large and its roots go deep into history. Already in the sixteenth century many people in the then Spice Islands had come to know the Lord and had formed strong indigenous churches. In other countries the churches may be more recent and not as large as in Indonesia.

A friend of mine working in Jordan has a wide ministry throughout the Middle East. He informed me, 'In every country of this area we are now seeing growing numbers of Muslims becoming believers in Jesus Christ as their Lord and Saviour.'

In many of these countries Muslim converts have to remain secret believers, for otherwise they would be killed. They may meet in small groups very secretly and few people will know about such conversions from Islam to Christian faith. But more and more Muslims are coming to know Jesus Christ. No longer is Christian witness apparently fruitless. Even in the countries of the Arabian peninsula, people are converting. Through the widespread use of computers and modern media, they are coming to know about other religions. No longer is Islam their only option. Now they can compare their experience of Islam and their Muslim society with the Christian faith and what Jesus offers his followers.

A considerable minority of Muslims today have become somewhat disillusioned with both the faith and practice of Islam in their countries. The extremism and violence of Islamists is repugnant to them. In contrast, the life, teaching, relationships and sacrificial death of Jesus proves very attractive. The life-giving resurrection of Jesus will also appeal in a special way.

'I am the first Christian in my people since the time of the Nestorians almost a thousand years ago. But now there are fifty of us,' announced one man after another in the testimony evenings. Numbers varied from fifty to about five hundred, but it was clear that new churches were becoming established in many of the North Caucasus ethnic groups. My wife and I had the privilege of giving Bible teaching at two conferences for Christian workers in the North Caucasus. It was exciting to meet and talk with each of the Christian leaders who gave their testimonies. Again and again in our ignorance we had to confess to each other that we had never previously heard of many of the peoples these sisters and brothers came from – various ethnic groups in Dagestan, Chechnya, Ossetia, Kabardino-Balkaria, and so on. But God knew them and was at work among them.

Having trained and worked as a Russian interpreter when I was younger, I have always had a special interest in the countries of the former Soviet Union. It was therefore a special privilege to be invited to minister in these North Caucasus conferences. But I have also been very grateful for the opportunity of ministering in some of the countries of Central Asia.

When I first went to Uzbekistan there were many Russian Christians, but still not a single Uzbek believer. Then back in the early 1990s I was invited to teach in a large Russian church, many hours east of Moscow by train, and there I met the first Uzbek Christian. She was a middle-aged lady, dynamic and strong-willed although sometimes not very tactful in personal relationships. But God has used her in his service. In his grace God has worked in wonderful ways and now there are several thousand Uzbek Christians.

Two years later, this lady invited my wife and me to come to Tashkent to teach in a conference for Uzbek Christians. It was held in a former Communist holiday centre for the party elite, but the centre was nevertheless somewhat dilapidated. When we tried to open our bedroom window, the whole window with its frame swung out into the darkness. The staircase from our top-floor room was unlit and totally dark in the evenings. Each step was of a different height and by no means flat, so we held on to each other for dear life as we climbed or descended the stairs. And the manholes in the road were uncovered and unmarked – very dangerous! The centre was located next to a disused uranium mine which was unguarded and open for everyone to walk into.

But the confident faith and inner joy of the Uzbek believers made the conference unforgettable. We found it difficult to remember that each of these Christians had only recently come to faith, for their spiritual maturity was impressive.

When I first visited Kazakhstan, communism still reigned with an iron fist. There were many Russian Christians, but only about a dozen Kazakh believers in the whole country. I knew that a former student of mine and her husband were quietly working in the capital city, translating the Bible into Kazakh. When it was published, it was soon accepted as the most beautiful Kazakh literature of all time. The Government therefore placed copies in all public libraries and in every primary school throughout the country.

I knew my friends' address, but had no idea how to find it. I duly got a bus to their housing area with one block of identical grey cement flats next to another. There seemed no rhyme nor reason why the different blocks had been given their particular numbers. But eventually I found number 113, wandered round it until I found the right staircase, climbed it and finally found their flat. I rang the bell and waited.

'Is it really possible? I can't believe it! What on earth are you doing in Alma Ata?' (at that time Almaty, the capital city of Kazakhstan, was called Alma Ata). Brunhilde was amazed to see me. In those days it was still very rare for a foreigner to visit Kazakhstan and she knew that it would have been very difficult for me to find her flat, for in those days no-one was willing to give a stranger directions.

Witness among the Kazakhs was perilous then. Since that time the Soviet Union has collapsed, the countries of Central Asia have gained their independence and Christian witness has multiplied. Today there are many thousands of believers among the Kazakh people.

To a lesser extent the Christian church has also grown among the Kyrgyz and other Central Asian peoples. Today official opposition is becoming ever more intense and the Christians face increasingly difficult situations, but the church among these Muslim peoples is now strong and continues to grow.

In the Indian subcontinent, new movements among Muslims can be found. In northern Bangladesh a large contextualized Christian church has emerged, using Muslim external forms but with Christian content and teaching. In their churches men do not sit together with women, the worship follows the outward patterns of Muslim salat and a month of fasting is observed. But Jesus Christ lives firmly in the centre of everything, in accordance with the Bible. In India too, there is a smaller movement along similar lines, but most Muslim converts join the traditional churches just like everyone else.

In Africa and in Western nations, Muslims and Christians are meeting each other more and more closely. Inevitably this leads to a movement in both directions. Growing numbers of white Europeans are joining Islam and we hear much about this on the media and in Muslim publications. At the same time a similar number of Muslims are becoming Christians, but this can be quite dangerous for those involved, so we hear less about it. With their apparent bias in favour of ethnic minorities and the non-Christian faiths, the media rarely mention the fact that Muslims are coming to faith in Jesus Christ.

As observed in chapter 4, Iranians are particularly open to the gospel of Jesus and are turning to him for salvation and new life. But Pakistanis, Afghans and others are also finding their way to life in Christ.

Perhaps the most encouraging movement to the Christian faith is happening in North Africa. Some twenty years ago in Algeria a few of the original Berber inhabitants of Algeria began to follow Jesus Christ. Since then their churches have multiplied and the Christian faith has spread not only among their fellow Berbers, but also into the majority Arab population. Persecution is increasing, but the power of the Holy Spirit is stronger and the Christians remain amazingly bold.

My wife and I have both had the privilege of helping in the teaching and training of Christian leaders in Algeria. Their enthusiasm for the Lord shows on their faces as one shares and the occasional 'Hallelujah' punctuates the teaching. Is this the first mass movement to Christ in North Africa since the time of Muhammad?

'We have three aims for our movement,' one of their leaders informed me. 'The first is that everybody in our province should have heard the gospel so clearly that they have made a definite, intelligent decision for or against Jesus.'

I was challenged. I could not think of any church in Britain which has as its aim that everyone in their county should have heard the gospel clearly in this way.

'This first aim is virtually complete now,' he continued. 'Our second aim is to plant churches all over Algeria. And we want churches not only among our own Kabyle [Berber] people, but also among the Arabs and other ethnic peoples.' He then told me that they had made a start with this second aim, but there remained much still to be done.

'Our third aim is to take the gospel in mission to all the Arabic-speaking nations around us in North Africa and the Middle East. We have begun to send mission teams on visits to some of these countries,' he explained, 'but we have not yet sent any long-term missionaries. Hopefully the time will soon come when we can do more work into other countries around us.'

I thought to myself, What an advantage these Algerian Christians have in mission to the central lands of Islam! They speak Arabic perfectly, know the culture from within and have fewer immigration problems than we do. God is surely at work in our day! Let us praise God and pray accordingly.

Although the Muslim fortress seems impregnable with its thick stone walls, our apparently ineffective little arrows are reinforced by the power of God's Holy Spirit. Cracks have begun to show – some large and some still quite small. As we witness as fellow workers with God's Spirit, let us pray that the castle may yield to the gracious love of God through Jesus the Messiah, Saviour and incarnate revelation of God himself. To him be the glory!

APPENDIX

Three things that Muslim converts have in common

'Most Muslim converts to Christianity normally share three things in common,' stated one well-known and experienced Christian worker among Muslims. While this statement is a generalization (my experience of Muslim converts in one part of Indonesia would classify as a major exception to this rule) his teaching points us nevertheless to a reality which we all need to look out for. And we can pray accordingly.

1. A long-term relationship with a Christian they respect

In these days when mass media play such a vital part in all forms of communication, it is good to be reminded that face-to-face personal relationships remain of crucial importance too. The use of mass media like the internet[1] should in no way be placed in conflict with the more personal interactions of Christians with their Muslim friends. The two must go hand in hand.

Again and again, the testimonies of Muslim converts underline the vital role played by their friendship with some particular Christian. In this way the Muslim can watch the gospel of Jesus Christ being incarnated in the life of the Christian. What does it mean to live as a Christian? What difference does faith in Jesus Christ make in situations of pain and suffering? How will it affect Muslims' relationships with other people if they become followers of Christ? How will they fit into the warm fellowship and love of the Christian church if they are forced out of the community of the people of Islam because of their faith in Jesus? These questions stand out in the potential convert's thinking. They represent very practical, down-to-earth issues and Muslims need visible, tangible models to demonstrate what it would be like if they were to leave Islam and become followers of Jesus Christ.

In various countries I have heard similar testimonies from Muslim converts. They tell how they gradually became friendly with a particular Christian. After some while they accepted the invitation to read the New Testament with their Christian friend, so week by week they grew in their understanding of the Christian faith. Finally they came to the point where they knew they had to make a definite decision for or against Jesus. But the cost of becoming a Christian stood like a battering ram against any possibility of turning to the Lord. They knew how they would at the very least be rejected by their family and their society, probably meaning that they would also lose their job or their possibility of further education. So they felt unwilling to face such enormous suffering and decided against following Jesus. In rejecting Jesus, they also felt embarrassed to meet their Christian friend again, so they broke that relationship too.

After a considerable time in which this particular Muslim and Christian never saw each other any more, suddenly and unexpectedly they bumped into each other again in the market or on the street. Humanly speaking, this meeting was totally by chance and, in the context of a major city, quite improbable. But God has his plans for us all!

'Fancy meeting you again!' the Muslim would then exclaim. 'Actually, I was just thinking recently about our friendship and those fascinating times we used to have together reading, discussing and praying.' And so the whole process begins again with weekly Bible study together. After some while the Muslim again gets to the stage of knowing he has to make a decision, and this time God bursts into his life with the gift of grace and new life. Once or twice I have even heard such stories where the Muslim has only come to faith in Jesus at the third bite of the cherry.

Patience and endurance will be key requirements as we allow our friends the ongoing opportunity to learn bit by bit the glories of Jesus Christ and his work of salvation on our behalf.

Deep personal friendship allows us to share very personally with people about all areas of life and about controversial issues of belief. As friends we can be more open with Muslims in a way which could be dangerous with strangers. Of course we need to be very discerning to know who is truly reliable as a friend.

2. A serious reading of at least part of the New Testament

We believe that the Bible is God's written Word and revelation. In Islam it is God's will which is revealed in the Qur'an. In the Bible, however, God speaks directly to people and reveals not only his will, but also himself so that we can form a new relationship with him through Jesus Christ by his Holy Spirit. So the Bible is like a personal letter written to us by God himself.

While it is true that God by his Spirit often speaks directly to people through the written word of the Bible, often Muslims require a Christian to explain its contents to them and help them to understand its meaning and its applications. We may see an example of this in the New Testament story of the Ethiopian eunuch and the apostle Philip (see Acts 8:26–40). This top official's reply gives the Christian church a fundamental principle for the use of the Bible in evangelistic ministry. 'How can I [understand what I'm reading],' he said, 'unless someone explains it to me?' (Acts

8:31). So it is still today in witness among Muslims. We often need to stand alongside and explain the Bible when they are willing to read it. In this way we can apply the Scripture to them and answer their questions.

Without a serious reading of at least part of the New Testament, and particularly the Gospels, Muslims may fail to be convinced that our witness carries the authority of God himself and his revealed Word. They are brought up to revere their scripture, holding the Qur'an in the highest possible esteem. This may be seen in the exceedingly careful way they handle the Qur'an, never putting it on the ground and usually carrying it wrapped in a neat clean cloth to preserve it from any contaminating dirt or dust.

As Christians we need also to make it abundantly clear that our faith is not just based on our own personal experience or what we consider to be intelligent and convincing. Our testimony should also be based on the written book of God, his inspired revelation to humankind. And we can trust that the Holy Spirit will speak through the revealed Word of God.

It is largely true that most Muslim converts to faith in Christ will have wrestled with the New Testament and seen something of the glory of the Lord through what they have read. Sometimes as Christians we may have lost the sense of amazement and wonder at the glory of God's Word. We have read and heard the Bible so often that its brilliance no longer strikes us. But when people have no biblical background at all and come fresh to the New Testament, it often bowls them over with its wonderful revelation of the life, relationships, teachings, death and resurrection of Jesus. Then the theological wisdom and truths of the Epistles stand alongside the exceedingly relevant and holy ethical standards of God. More modern Westernized Muslims may also be surprised to note the New Testament's strong teaching on justice, ecological care for creation and the equality of women. The Muslim may therefore find their former study of the Qur'an seems quite insipid in comparison. No wonder many Muslim leaders forbid their people to read the Bible!

3. Miracles

'When the authorities discovered that I had become a Christian, they arrested me,' Jemail shared with me as we drove from the church to lunch together. 'Of course, my family and friends had all already rejected me and thrown me out of the home, so I felt very alone and abandoned. Happily, my Christian friends and the church have befriended and supported me wonderfully.' He looked so ordinary in rather poor everyday Western-style clothing. His thin, brown-skinned face showed no emotion and his deep-set eyes looked out impassively on a potentially hostile world.

Jemail had been put into a re-education establishment with the stated intention that he should return to Islam. There he had been subjected to a harsh regime of Muslim indoctrination, sleep deprivation and poor food. He had witnessed fellow inmates cave in one by one under the authorities' pressure and the constant brainwashing from long hours of Islamic teaching and activity. 'If you don't return to Islam,' he was told, 'you will remain here for however long it takes.'

However, Jemail's faith remained firm under every pressure. There seemed no escape, but he still refused to deny his new-found Saviour.

Finally, one day, he was hauled before the authorities again and informed, 'If you won't return to Islam, we shall force you. We are going to give you electric shock treatment to your brain so that you will not be able to remember what you learned about Jesus and the Christian religion.'

Through this electric shock treatment he lost all memory of his childhood and youth. Much of what he had learned at school had been eliminated from his mind.

But wonderfully, in the grace of God, he still clearly remembered his conversion and what he had learned about Jesus. He still rejoiced in the Lord and his salvation. In our conversation together he remained quietly lucid in telling us his story and sharing his testimony as a Christian.

Finally Jemail had run away from the re-education centre and was now on the run from the police. His pastor and the leaders of his church had taken him in despite the danger and were supporting him financially and in every other way. It would seem that the only possible future for Jemail would involve him being smuggled out of the country to live as an asylum seeker abroad. The cost of becoming a Christian can be high.

Facing the dangers and suffering inherent in becoming a Christian, Muslims need some very definite evidence that God will not only give his salvation and Holy Spirit to them, but also that he is able and willing to work powerfully on their behalf. The power of Islam against them must be out-matched by the miraculous power of God to protect them.

In Jemail's country we knew of three girls who had been poisoned by their mother because they began to show inter-est in Christian things. Fierce persecution of converts from Islam is sadly common in many Muslim nations. Even where the death penalty for apostasy is not always practised, many are thrown out of their family and home. They may well find it impossible to get further education or a job, so life can become very hard. Local Christians have often had bad experiences of young Muslim men pretending to become

Christians in order to marry a particular girl, but then after marriage they have reverted to Islam and taken their wife with them. In this way the churches have lost some of their girls, and Christian parents are often now unwilling to allow their daughters to marry a former Muslim. So the new convert from Islam is barred from marrying a Christian girl, but he does not want a Muslim wife either. In such circumstances, marriage becomes a problem for younger unmarried converts. Muslims are then strongly in need of a miracle from God to encourage them as they turn to Christ.

As we have seen in chapter 5, God commonly works some miracle for the potential Muslim convert to strengthen them in their resolve to become followers of Jesus Christ. Sometimes this takes the form of a healing miracle or the casting out of demonic spirits, but more normally God speaks to such people through a vision or dream.

For example, Ismail tells of his going to Mecca on the hajj. He duly joined the throngs of people walking round the holy Kaaba in the traditional ritual of the pilgrimage, which Muhammad himself performed when he conquered Mecca.

Ismail remembers clearly the feelings he had as he performed the hajj. 'The sun was shining brightly, as is usual in Mecca. Then suddenly I saw the whole sky lit up by a brilliant cross from one end of the horizon to the other. Even with the tropical sun and the bright blue sky, the glory of the cross outshone it all. It stood out, almost blinding me with its intensity.' A long pause ensued as he remembered this God-given miracle which had changed his whole life. 'Then a voice spoke clearly to me, saying "You will not find me here" and I knew immediately that I had to search for God in some other way.'

The fact that the vision came in the shape of a brilliant cross made it obvious to Ismail that the way God had chosen was through Jesus and the Christian belief that the cross has brought forgiveness and redemption. Knowing the reality of God through a miraculous vision of this nature gave Ismail the confidence to become a Christian despite the persecution and pressures that would naturally follow his conversion from Islam.

God remains the sovereign Lord who can work in our lives and on our behalf in whatever ways he wishes. He has the freedom to minister to Muslims in whatever ways he sees best. He has a wonderful way of adapting his means to fit our particular backgrounds, beliefs and cultures.

To conclude

It is commonly true that many Muslim converts have these three things in common – a long-term relationship or friendship with a Christian whom they respect, a serious reading of at least part of the New Testament and the experience of a miracle which they associate with Jesus Christ and the Christian faith. We rejoice in growing numbers of Muslims who are turning to Christ in this way these days both in the West and elsewhere. But let us also work and pray that the Holy Spirit will add to their number so that we may witness the reality of his purpose that not only will 'all Israel . . . be saved', but also that 'the full number of the Gentiles' (Romans 11:25–26) will come into faith in Jesus Christ to the glory of the Father.

NOTES

Introduction
1. For a more graphic description of our evangelistic sorties in the Singapore night markets, see Goldsmith, M. (1997), *Life's Tapestry* (Authentic Lifestyle).

Chapter 3
1. For further study of the relation between the term Allah and the biblical Creator, see Goldsmith, M. (2008), *What About Other Faiths?* (Hodder Revised Edition).

Chapter 5
1. For a more detailed account of two such Muslim shamans in South Thailand, see Goldsmith, M. (1997), *Life's Tapestry* (Authentic Lifestyle).

Chapter 6
1. For an excellent description of Muslims in Britain, see Snow, J. and Lewis, P. (2007), *Young, British and Muslim* (Continuum).

Chapter 9
1. For an excellent description of the radicalization of Islam in the younger generation in Britain, see Husain, E. (2006), *The Islamist* (Penguin).

Chapter 11
1. Acts 9:27–29; 13:46; 14:3; 18:26; 19:8; 28:31; Ephesians 6:19–20; 1 Thessalonians 2:2.

Appendix
1. For further discussion of the use of modern media in contemporary mission, see chapter 7 of Goldsmith, M. (2006), *Get a Grip on Mission: The Challenge of a Changing World* (Inter-Varsity Press).

OTHER PUBLICATIONS BY MARTIN AND ELIZABETH GOLDSMITH

By Martin Goldsmith

Any Complaints? Blame God!: God's Message for Today – Habakkuk the Prophet Speaks (Authentic, 2008)

Choices: Learning to Hear God's Voice (Authentic, 2007)

Get a Grip on Mission: The Challenge of a Changing World (IVP and OMF, 2006)

Life's Tapestry: Reflections and Insights from My Life (Authentic, 1997)

Matthew and Mission: The Gospel through Jewish Eyes (Paternoster, 2001)

What About Other Faiths?: Is Jesus Christ the Only Way to God? (Hodder, 1989, 2008)

Who Is My Neighbour? (Authentic, 2002)

By Elizabeth Goldsmith

Against All Odds: God at Work in an Impossible Situation (Authentic and OMF, 2007)

God Can Be Trusted (Authentic, 1974, 1996)

Roots and Wings: Five Generations and Their Influence (OM Publishing, 1998)